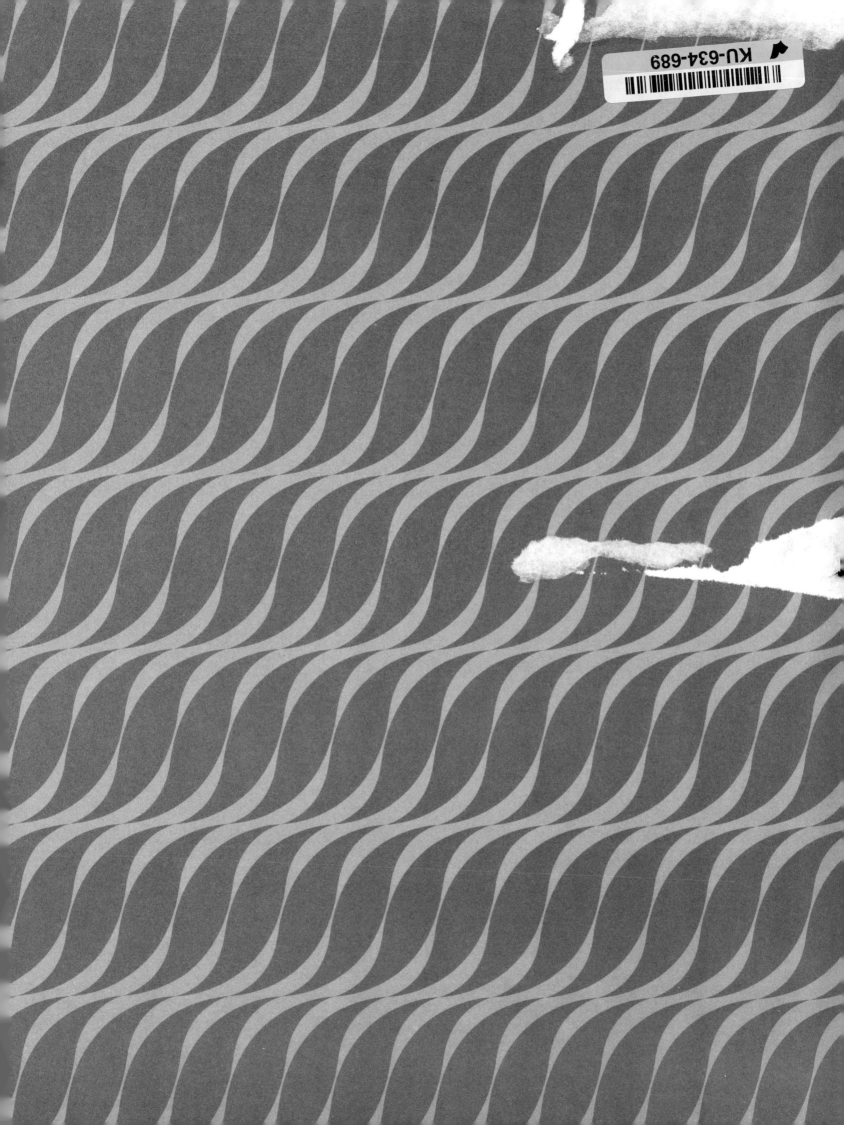

pasta
sauces

pasta sauces

100 sauces, starters, salads and soups

jeni wright

southwater

This edition is published by Southwater

Distributed in the UK by
The Manning Partnership
251–253 London Road East
Batheaston
Bath BA1 7RL
UK
tel. (0044) 01225 852 727
fax. (0044) 01225 852 852

Distributed in the USA by
Ottenheimer Publishing
5 Park Center Court
Suite 300
Owing Mills MD 2117–5001
USA
tel. (001) 410 902 9100
fax. (001) 410 902 7210

Distributed in Australia by
Sandstone Publishing
Unit 1, 360 Norton Street
Leichhardt
New South Wales 2040
Australia
tel. (0061) 2 9560 7888
fax. (0061) 2 9560 7488

Distributed in New Zealand by
Five Mile Press NZ
PO Box 33–1071
Takapuna
Auckland 9
New Zealand
tel. (0064) 9 4444 144
fax. (0064) 9 4444 518

Southwater is an imprint of Anness Publishing Limited
© 1999, 2000 Anness Publishing Limited

1 3 5 7 9 10 8 6 4 2

PUBLISHER: Joanna Lorenz
EXECUTIVE EDITOR: Linda Fraser
EDITOR: Susannah Blake
DESIGNER: Patrick McCleavey
PHOTOGRAPHERS: William Lingwood (recipes) and Janine Hosegood (techniques and cutouts)
FOOD FOR PHOTOGRAPHY: Lucy McKelvie and Kate Jay (recipes) and Annabel Ford (techniques)
EDITORIAL READER: Diane Ashmore
PRODUCTION CONTROLLER: Yolande Denny

Previously published as part of a larger compendium *The Pasta Bible*

NOTES
For all recipes, quantities are given in both metric and imperial measures and, where appropriate, measures are also given in standard cups and spoons. Follow one set, but not a mixture, because they are not interchangeable.

Standard spoon and cup measures are level.
1 tsp = 5ml, 1 tbsp = 15ml, 1 cup = 250ml/8fl oz

Australian standard tablespoons are 20ml. Australian readers should use 3 tsp in place of 1 tbsp for measuring small quantities of gelatine, cornflour, salt, etc.

Medium eggs are used unless otherwise stated.

CONTENTS

Introduction

Pasta is one of the most popular foods in the world today and is perfect for any occasion, from impromptu suppers and family meals to sophisticated dinner parties. It can be served hot with any number of sauces, cooled and combined with a dressing to make a salad, or simmered gently in soup.

Pasta sauces needn't be complicated or time-consuming to make, they can be thick or thin, chunky or smooth, rich and rustic, and even fresh and healthy. The simplest sauces can be made in seconds and may consist of a drizzle of olive oil and some crushed garlic, while rich meat sauces need long, slow simmering to bring out the flavours. Pasta salads are a delicious option. The warm pasta can be simply tossed with the most minimal of ingredients, such as olive oil, garlic and fresh herbs and served or combined with meat, vegetables and a piquant to make a summer lunch dish.

Hearty pasta soups can be a complete meal in a bowl, while a traditional Italian broth made with pasta shapes or little pieces of stuffed tortellini makes for a great pick-me-up if you are feeling under-the-weather.

Pasta Sauces

In Italy, the sauce is added sparingly. It is usually tossed with the freshly drained hot pasta in the kitchen, and the mixture is then brought to the table in one large bowl. In other countries, a little more sauce is usual and plain pasta is often divided among the bowls or plates and then the sauce spooned on top. Alternatively, the pasta can be tossed with the sauce and then served in individual portions.

Choosing the right sauce is all important when eating pasta. Some regional dishes are always made with the same pasta shape. *Bucatini all'Amatriciana* and *Penne all'Arrabbiata* are classic Roman recipes, for example, and it is rare to see them served with anything other than the named pasta. The same applies to *Tagliatelle alla Bolognese* from Emilia-Romagna and *Trenette con Pesto* from Genoa. These classics are few and far between, however, and with the ever-increasing number of different shapes on the market it may seem difficult to know which sauces and shapes will complement each other.

Happily, there are no rigid rules, and common sense usually prevails. Heavy sauces with large chunks of meat are unlikely to go well with thin spaghettini or tagliolini, simply because the chunks will slide off, so these types of sauces are always served with wide noodles, such as tagliatelle, or with short tubular shapes, such as penne, fusilli and rigatoni, which will hold the sauce much better.

In the south of Italy, olive oil is used for cooking rather than butter, so sauces tend to be made with olive oil and they are usually served with the dried plain durum wheat pasta, such as spaghetti, that is also popular in the south. These long, thin shapes are traditionally served with tomato and seafood sauces, most of which are made with olive oil, and with light vegetable sauces. Spaghetti and vermicelli are also ideal vehicles for minimalist sauces like *Aglio e Olio* (garlic and olive oil) from Rome or *Spaghetti al Limone*. Grated cheese is not normally used in these sauces, nor is it sprinkled over them.

In the North, butter and cream are popular ingredients for sauces, and not surprisingly these go well with the egg pasta that is made there, especially fresh home-made egg pasta. Fresh pasta absorbs butter and cream, making the sauce cling to it. Butter and cream also go well with tomato sauces and are delicious when served with short shapes, such as penne, farfalle and fusilli.

Grated cheese, such as Parmesan and Pecorino, is often tossed with pasta and sauce at the last moment, as well as being sprinkled over individual servings at the table.

Combining the Pasta and Sauce

Recipes vary in the way they combine the sauce and pasta. Some add the sauce to the pasta, while others add the pasta to the sauce.

1 After draining and reserving a little of the cooking water, tip the pasta into a large, warmed bowl. Immediately pour the hot sauce over the pasta and quickly, but gently, toss together.

2 If the pasta is not moist enough, add a little of the pasta cooking water. Some recipes call for extra butter or oil to be added at this stage, others have grated cheese tossed with the pasta and sauce.

3 Use two large spoons or forks for tossing. Lift the pasta and swirl it around, making sure you have scooped it up from the bottom of the bowl, coating every piece of pasta evenly in sauce.

4 Some recipes call for the pasta to be returned to the cooking pan, to be combined with oil or butter and seasonings. A sauce may be added at this stage too, but care should be taken not to overcook the pasta when it is reheated.

Some classic dishes, such as Bucatini all'Amatriciana (above), are usually served with the named pasta, but there's no real reason why you shouldn't substitute tagliatelle or spaghetti.

Pasta Salads

Freshly cooked pasta makes the perfect salad ingredient; it soaks up dressings and absorbs the flavour of other ingredients well, so salads made with pasta are always moist and full of flavour. Any pasta shape can be used for salads, although open shapes such as conchiglie and lumaconi and hollow tubes like penne are particularly good because they trap the dressing and other ingredients.

Pasta salads are generally very quick and easy to make and can be as simple or as complicated as you like – whether you simply toss the cooked pasta with a handful of chopped raw ingredients and mix with a bottled dressing or a spoonful of mayonnaise, or take a little longer to make a special recipe, such as Seafood Salad or Pasta Salade Niçoise.

Pasta Soups

Throughout Italy, pasta is eaten in soups, which range from clear broths to more filling soups with chunky pieces of pasta and vegetables, meat or fish.

Broths usually include tiny pasta shapes, such as risoni, or larger stuffed pasta, such as tortellini, and are often served as a pick-me-up for adults who are not feeling well. If you stay in an Italian hospital, you are likely to be served *Pastina in Brodo*.

Adding a handful of pasta to a soup or broth provides extra substance and can create a soup that is filling enough for a meal. In Italy, *Tortellini in Brodo* is often served on its own or with bread for an evening meal when the main meal of the day has been at lunchtime.

Eating Pasta

Opinions vary as to whether pasta should be eaten from a plate or a bowl. There are no strict rules, so you can serve it on either. Large, shallow soup plates seem the ideal compromise, and setting each warmed soup plate on a large, cold underplate makes for easy carrying.

If the recipe recommends extra Parmesan or Pecorino for serving, grate the cheese just before the meal and hand it round in a bowl with a small spoon so that people can help themselves. Salt and pepper mills should also be on the table for those who like to adjust the seasoning.

Pasta is traditionally eaten with a single fork. Spaghetti and other long shapes should not be difficult to manage if they have been well tossed with the sauce. The trick is to twizzle only a small amount around the fork at a time (right).

How to Cook and Serve Pasta

It is very easy to cook pasta properly, but without care and attention it is equally easy to cook it badly. A few simple guidelines need to be observed if pasta is to be at its best. Once you have mastered these, you will be able to cook pasta successfully every time, no matter whether it is dried, home-made or bought fresh.

1 Synchronize sauce and pasta

Before starting to cook either sauce or pasta, read through the recipe carefully. It is important to know which needs to be cooked for the longest time – sometimes it is the pasta and sometimes the sauce. The sauce can often be made ahead of time and reheated, whereas pasta is better when freshly cooked.

2 Use a big pan

There needs to be plenty of room for the pasta to move around as it cooks. The best type of pan is a tall, lightweight stainless steel pasta cooking pot with its own in-built draining pan. The handles on either side ensure easy and safe lifting and draining. If you do not have one of these special pans, use the largest saucepan you have and a large stainless steel colander.

3 Use a large quantity of water

The recommended amount is 5 litres/8 pints water for every 450g/1lb pasta. If you are cooking less pasta than this, use at least 3 litres/5 pints water. If there is not enough water, the pasta shapes will stick together as they swell, resulting in gummy-textured pasta.

4 Get the water boiling

Before adding the pasta, the water should be at a fast rolling boil. The quickest way to do this is to boil water in the kettle, then pour it into the pasta pan, which should be set over a high heat. You may need as much as 2–3 kettlefuls, so keep the water in the pan simmering while you boil the kettle again.

5 Add enough salt

Pasta cooked without salt is more or less tasteless, and with insufficient salt it is hardly any better. The recommended amount is 25–30ml/1 1/2–2 tbsp salt for every 450g/1lb pasta. There is no need to use sea or rock salt; cooking salt is perfectly acceptable. Add the salt when the water is boiling and just before you are ready to add the pasta. The water will bubble furiously just as the salt is added, which is your cue to shoot in the pasta.

6 Tip in the pasta all at once

Try to get all of the pasta into the boiling water at the same time so that it will cook evenly and be ready at the same time. The quickest and easiest way is literally to shake it out of the packet or the bowl of the scales, covering the surface of the water as much as possible.

7 Return the water quickly to the boil

Once the pasta is submerged in the water, give it a brisk stir with a long-handled fork or spoon and then cover the pan tightly with the lid – this will help to bring the water back to the boil as quickly as possible. Once the water is boiling, lift off the lid, turn down the heat slightly and let the water simmer over a medium to high heat for the required cooking time.

8 Stir the pasta frequently during cooking

To prevent the pasta strands or shapes from sticking together, stir them frequently during cooking so they are kept constantly on the move. Use a long-handled wooden fork or spoon so you can stir right down to the bottom of the pan.

9 Drain carefully and thoroughly

If you have a pasta pot with an inner drainer, lift the draining pan up and out of the water. Shake the draining pan vigorously and stir the pasta well so that any water trapped in pasta shapes can drain out. Reserve a few ladlefuls of the pasta cooking water in case the pasta needs a little extra moistening when it is tossed with the sauce before serving.

Cooking Long Dried Pasta

1 For spaghetti you need to coil the pasta into the water. Take a handful at a time and dip it in the boiling water so that it touches the bottom of the pan.

2 As the spaghetti strands soften, coil them round using a wooden spoon or fork until they are all submerged.

Cooking Stuffed Pasta

1 Stuffed shapes require more gentle handling or they may break open, so stir them gently during cooking.

2 The best method of draining stuffed shapes after cooking is to lift them carefully out of the water with a large pasta scoop or slotted spoon.

When is it Cooked?

The Italian term *al dente* is used to describe pasta that is cooked to perfection. Literally translated this means "to the tooth", meaning that it should be firm to the bite, which is how Italians like their pasta. Dried pasta is always served *al dente*, whereas fresh pasta is made from a softer wheat and so is never as firm as dried, but it should still have some resistance to it. Overcooked pasta is limp and unpalatable and an Italian cook would not serve it.

To check that the pasta is ready, test frequently towards the end of the recommended cooking time by lifting out a piece with tongs, a pasta scoop or a slotted spoon and biting into it. When it is done to your liking, it is time to stop the cooking.

Serving and Presentation

When serving pasta, it is important to have your family and friends waiting at the table for the pasta, rather than the other way around. Pasta should be eaten as soon as it is cooked and tossed with the sauce, so invite everyone to sit down just before you are ready to drain the pasta.

In most cases, pasta and sauce are tossed together in a large serving bowl in the kitchen, and the bowl is then brought straight to the table. Each person is served straight from the bowl or, alternatively, the bowl is passed around the table for everyone to help themselves.

When you are serving pasta directly from the bowl, it looks most attractive if you retain a small ladleful of the sauce to put on top of the pasta after tossing.

To give the pasta a finishing touch, a little Parmesan or Pecorino cheese can be grated on top, or a few chopped fresh herbs, such as parsley or basil, can be sprinkled over. The choice of garnish depends on the dish and the cook, but as a general rule, cheese is never served

with fish and shellfish sauces. For guidance follow the garnishing instructions in individual recipes.

Occasionally, the pasta and sauce are divided among individual plates or bowls before serving – as is the practice in

restaurants. This is not the traditional custom in Italian homes, but it sometimes helps to get the pasta served quickly. It is an especially good idea when you are entertaining, because each serving can be given its own garnish (below).

Pasta Shapes

There are many hundreds of different types of pasta – both fresh and dried – that can be served with a sauce or in salads and soups. Long and short shapes are the most common, but there are also stuffed shapes and tiny shapes for use in soup. Among these, you will find some less well-known regional shapes and the more unusual and decorative designer shapes.

When buying dried pasta, choose one that is made using 100 per cent durum wheat. If you decant pasta shapes into storage jars, use up any remaining pasta before adding more from a new packet. Older pasta may take longer to cook than that from a fresher packet, and different brands of the same shape may not necessarily have the same cooking time.

When buying freshly made pasta, buy it on the day you need it; otherwise keep it in its wrapping and use it within 1–2 days of purchase (or according to the storage time given on the packet). Fresh pasta is made with egg, which shortens its storage time but, on the plus side, this increases its nutritional value and flavour, and gives the plain varieties a lovely yellow colour.

LONG PASTA / *PASTA LUNGA*

Dried long pasta in the form of spaghetti is probably the best-known pasta of all time, and was certainly one of the first types to be exported from Italy. Spaghetti is still very widely used, but nowadays there are many other varieties of long pasta that look and taste just as good, such as tagliatelle, linguine and *capelli d'angelo*.

Most dried long shapes are available in plain durum wheat only. The shapes made with egg (all'uovo) are very delicate, and

Clinging sauces made with olive oil, butter and cream are good with fresh egg and spinach-flavoured linguine.

are either packed in nests or compressed as waves. Fine long pasta, such as spaghetti, is far too delicate to be made with egg. Fresh long pasta, however, can be made with egg because it is not so brittle.

There are no hard-and-fast rules when matching pasta to sauce, so experiment with alternative varieties to add interest to your cooking, always remembering that long pasta is best served with either a thin, clinging sauce or a smooth, thick sauce.

If too thin and watery, the sauce will simply run off the long strands; if too chunky or heavy, the sauce will fall to the bottom of the bowl and you will be left with a bowl full of chunks and no pasta to eat it with. Clinging sauces made with olive oil, butter, cream, eggs, finely grated cheese and chopped fresh herbs are good with long pasta. When ingredients such as vegetables, fish and meat are added to a smooth thick sauce, they should be very finely chopped.

SHORT PASTA / *PASTA CORTA*

There are literally hundreds of different short pasta shapes, and new ones are constantly coming into our shops. Some people prefer short pasta simply because it is easier to cook and eat than long pasta. It also goes well with many different sauces and is perfect for salads with large pieces of meat, fish or vegetables. In most cases you can choose any shape you fancy, regardless of whether your sauce is chunky or a smooth tomato-, cream- or olive oil-based type. Exceptions are regional dishes that are traditionally cooked with a specific shape, such as *Penne all'Arrabbiata* from Lazio.

Conchiglie are particularly good in salads because they trap the dressing and other ingredients so well.

Short pasta is divided into two main groups. *Pasta secca* is factory-made, using durum wheat flour and water. This is by far the largest group, and you will find that most packets of dried pasta list only these two ingredients on the label. *Pasta all'uovo* is made with the addition of eggs. It is naturally a brighter yellow than *pasta secca* and has more nutritional value. Popular in the north of Italy, especially in Emilia-Romagna, *pasta all'uovo* has different properties from plain pasta and goes especially well with the rich creamy and meaty sauces associated with that part of Italy. It cooks slightly more quickly than plain durum wheat pasta and is less likely to become overcooked and soggy. Although it is more expensive than plain pasta, egg pasta is becoming more popular and therefore more widely available.

New flavours and colours of short pasta shapes are on the increase, too. For many years, tomato (*pomodoro*) and spinach (*verde*) were all that was available, but today there seems to be no end to

Capelli d'angelo a nidi is best served with a thin, clinging sauce or one that is smooth and thick.

Fusilli con spinaci are delicious served with a chunky vegetable sauce or in a refreshing summer salad.

the number of different colour and flavour combinations, ranging from garlic, chillies and herbs to beetroot, salmon, mushroom, squid ink and even chocolate. Often three colours (red, white and green) are packed together and labelled *tricolore*. Whole-wheat pasta, called *pasta integrale*, is made from durum wheat and other cereals. It is higher in fibre than plain durum wheat pasta and takes longer to cook.

STUFFED PASTA / *PASTA RIPIENA*
The most common dried stuffed pasta shapes are tortellini (little pies), a speciality of Bologna said to be modelled on the shape of Venus's navel. They are made from rounds or circles of pasta, so they look like little plump rings.

Dried tortellini are generally available with a wide choice of fillings – with meat (*alla carne*) or cheese (*ai formaggi*). The pasta may be plain or flavoured with spinach or tomato. They are very popular and most Italian cooks keep a packet or two of tortellini in the store cupboard for making *Tortellini in Brodo,* which is often served for an evening meal when the main

meal of the day has been at lunchtime. You can also be sure that *Tortellini in Brodo* will be served as a pick-me-up if ever a member of the family is unwell. They are also good boiled, then drained and tossed in melted butter and herbs or a cream, tomato or meat sauce.

Dried tortellini are traditionally simmered in clear beef or chicken stock until they swell and plump to make a satisfying soup.

Semi-dried tomato-flavoured cappelletti stuffed with sun-dried tomato filling are delicious tossed in melted butter and herbs.

Other stuffed shapes, such as cappelletti, ravioli and agnolotti, are more likely to be sold fresh than dried. The traditional stuffed shapes and fillings are often varied nowadays. A wide variety of fresh seasonal ingredients for the fillings, plus eye-catching colour combinations for both the pasta and the fillings make endless variations on the theme.

Risoni (top) and tubetti (above) are served in clear soups and broths.

DRIED PASTA FOR SOUP / *PASTINA*
Teeny-weeny pasta shapes are called *pastina* in Italian, and there are literally hundreds of different ones to choose from. They are mostly made from plain durum wheat, although you may find them made with egg and even flavoured with carrot or spinach.

The smallest and most plain *pasta per minestre* (pasta for soups) are like tiny grains. Some look like rice and are in fact called risi or risoni. The next size up are the ones that are most popular with children, including alfabeti and alfabetini (alphabet shapes), stelline and stellette (stars) and rotellini (tiny wagon wheels).

Another category of *pasta per ministre* consists of slightly larger shapes, more like miniature versions of familiar types of short pasta. Their names end in "ine", "ette" or "etti", denoting that they are the diminutive forms. These include conchigliette (little shells), farfalline and farfallette (little bows).

Five-colour chioccioloni is flavoured with squid ink, chocolate, tomato and porcini and is best served with a very simple sauce based on olive oil or butter.

Designer Pasta
Relative newcomers to the market are the pasta shapes that bear little or no resemblance to the traditional or regional Italian varieties. Many of these are made outside Italy and the ones made in Italy are often for export only.

Supermarkets and food halls, gourmet food shops, specialist delicatessens and even interior design shops are the best places to find these new shapes, which are often coloured and flavoured. Quality

varies enormously, and some of them have very disappointing textures and flavours. Others are more successful, especially the ones made by long-established Italian firms. They make a change from the more usual shapes and are often an interesting talking point, especially when you are entertaining.

Flavoured pasta is usually better served with a simple sauce, otherwise the flavour of the sauce and the pasta tend to fight one another.

Cream and Cheese Sauces

The northern Italians love both cream and cheese as an accompaniment to pasta. The unctuous texture of creamy sauce goes well with *pasta all'uovo*, pasta made with egg, and complements fresh pasta perfectly. The cream used in Italy is called *panna da cucina* (cream for cooking) and has a thin, almost runny, consistency and a slight tang. You can buy it fresh in Italy, but beyond its borders you are more likely to see long-life *panna da cucina* in delicatessens and specialist stores. Italian cheeses vary enormously in flavour and texture, which has given rise to an exciting range of classic and modern sauces. Thick and creamy mascarpone can create deliciously smooth, mild sauces, whereas distinctively flavoured cheeses, such as Gorgonzola, can introduce a tangy kick.

Cream and cheese can be used as the key ingredient in recipes such as *Vermicelli al Limone* or, alternatively, they can be combined with seasonal vegetables, such as asparagus and wild mushrooms, or more unusual ingredients, such as radicchio. Pasta with a cream or cheese sauce makes a good dinner party first course, but keep portions small, because flavours are rich.

Linguine al Prosciutto e Mascarpone

Linguine with Ham and Mascarpone

MASCARPONE CHEESE masquerades as cream in this recipe. Its thick, unctuous consistency makes it perfect for sauces. Have the water boiling, ready for the pasta, before you start making the sauce, because everything cooks so quickly.

INGREDIENTS

25g/1oz/2 tbsp butter

150g/5oz/³/4 cup mascarpone cheese

*90g/3¹/2oz cooked ham, cut into
   thin strips*

30ml/2 tbsp milk

*45ml/3 tbsp freshly grated Parmesan
   cheese, plus extra to serve*

500g/1¹/4lb fresh linguine

salt and ground black pepper

Serves 6

1 Melt the butter in a medium saucepan, add the mascarpone, ham and milk and stir well over a low heat until the mascarpone has melted. Add 15ml/1 tbsp of the grated Parmesan and plenty of pepper and stir well.

2 Cook the pasta in a large saucepan of salted boiling water for 2–3 minutes until *al dente*.

3 Drain the cooked pasta well and tip it into a warmed bowl. Pour the sauce over the pasta, add the remaining Parmesan and toss well.

4 Taste for seasoning and serve the pasta immediately, with more ground black pepper and extra grated Parmesan handed separately.

Farfalle alla Crema di Gorgonzola

Farfalle with Gorgonzola Cream

SWEET AND SIMPLE, this sauce has a nutty tang from the blue cheese. It is also good with long pasta, such as spaghetti or trenette.

INGREDIENTS

350g/12oz/3 cups dried farfalle

*175g/6oz Gorgonzola cheese, any rind
   removed, diced*

*150ml/¹/4 pint/²/3 cup panna da cucina or
   double cream*

pinch of granulated sugar

*10ml/2 tsp finely chopped fresh sage, plus
   fresh sage leaves (some whole, some
   shredded) to garnish*

salt and ground black pepper

Serves 4

1 Cook the pasta until *al dente*: 8–10 minutes or according to the instructions on the packet.

2 Meanwhile, put the Gorgonzola and cream in a medium saucepan. Add the sugar and plenty of ground black pepper and heat gently, stirring frequently, until the cheese has melted. Remove the pan from the heat.

3 Drain the cooked pasta well and return it to the pan in which it was cooked. Pour the sauce into the pan with the pasta.

4 Add the chopped sage to the pasta and toss over a medium heat until the pasta is evenly coated. Taste for seasoning, adding salt if necessary, then divide among four warmed bowls. Garnish each portion with sage and serve immediately.

Pipe Rigate ai Piselli e Prosciutto

Pipe Rigate with Peas and Ham

3 Add about half the cream, increase the heat to high and let the cream bubble, stirring constantly, until it thickens and coats the peas. Remove from the heat, stir in the prosciutto and taste for seasoning.

4 Cook the pasta according to the instructions on the packet. Tip into a colander and drain well.

5 Immediately melt the remaining butter with the cream in the pan in which the pasta was cooked. Add the pasta and toss over a medium heat until it is evenly coated. Pour in the sauce, toss lightly to mix with the pasta and heat through. Serve immediately, sprinkled with fresh herbs.

PRETTILY FLECKED WITH PINK and green, this is a lovely dish for a spring or summer supper party.

INGREDIENTS

25g/1oz/2 tbsp butter

15ml/1 tbsp olive oil

150–175g/5–6oz/1¼–1½ cups frozen peas, thawed

1 garlic clove, crushed

150ml/¼ pint/⅔ cup chicken stock, dry white wine or water

30ml/2 tbsp chopped fresh flat leaf parsley

175ml/6fl oz/¾ cup panna da cucina or double cream

115g/4oz prosciutto crudo (Parma ham), shredded

350g/12oz/3 cups dried pipe rigate

salt and ground black pepper

chopped fresh herbs, to garnish

Serves 4

1 Melt half the butter with the olive oil in a medium saucepan until foaming. Add the thawed frozen peas and the crushed garlic to the pan, followed by the chicken stock, wine or water.

2 Sprinkle in the chopped parsley and add salt and pepper to taste. Cook over a medium heat, stirring frequently, for 5–8 minutes or until most of the liquid has been absorbed.

COOK'S TIPS

• *Prosciutto is quite expensive, but it tastes very good in this dish. To cut the cost you could use ordinary cooked ham or pancetta.*

• *If you can't get pipe rigate, use conchiglie or orecchiette instead, all of which trap the peas.*

Fusilli di Bosco
Fusilli with Wild Mushrooms

A VERY RICH DISH WITH AN earthy flavour and lots of garlic, this makes an ideal main course for vegetarians, especially if it is followed by a crisp green salad.

INGREDIENTS

1/2 x 275g/10oz jar wild mushrooms in olive oil
25g/1oz/2 tbsp butter
225g/8oz/2 cups fresh wild mushrooms, sliced if large
5ml/1 tsp finely chopped fresh thyme
5ml/1 tsp finely chopped fresh marjoram or oregano, plus extra herbs to serve
4 garlic cloves, crushed
350g/12oz/3 cups fresh or dried fusilli
200ml/7fl oz/scant 1 cup panna da cucina or double cream
salt and ground black pepper
Serves 4

1 Drain about 15ml/1 tbsp of the oil from the mushrooms into a medium saucepan. Slice or chop the bottled mushrooms into bite-size pieces, if they are large.

2 Add the butter to the oil in the pan and place over a low heat until sizzling. Add the bottled and the fresh mushrooms, the chopped herbs and the garlic, with salt and pepper to taste. Simmer over a medium heat, stirring frequently, for about 10 minutes or until the fresh mushrooms are soft and tender. Meanwhile, cook the pasta in salted boiling water according to the instructions on the packet.

3 As soon as the mushrooms are cooked, increase the heat to high and toss the mixture with a wooden spoon to drive off any excess liquid. Pour in the cream and bring to the boil, stirring, then taste and add more salt and pepper if needed.

4 Drain the pasta and tip it into a warmed bowl. Pour the sauce over the pasta and toss well. Serve immediately, sprinkled with extra fresh herb leaves.

Farfalle Verdi e Rosa

Pink and Green Farfalle

IN THIS MODERN RECIPE, pink prawns and green courgettes combine prettily with cream and pasta bows to make a substantial main course. Serve with crusty Italian rolls or chunks of warm ciabatta bread.

INGREDIENTS

50g/2oz/¼ cup butter
2–3 spring onions, very thinly sliced on
 the diagonal
350g/12oz courgettes, thinly sliced on
 the diagonal
60ml/4 tbsp dry white wine
300g/11oz/2¾ cups dried farfalle
75ml/5 tbsp crème fraîche
225g/8oz/1⅓ cups peeled cooked
 prawns, thawed and thoroughly dried
 if frozen
15ml/1 tbsp finely chopped fresh marjoram
 or flat leaf parsley, or a mixture
salt and ground black pepper
Serves 4

1 Melt the butter in a large saucepan, add the spring onions and cook over a low heat, stirring frequently, for about 5 minutes until softened. Add the courgettes, with salt and pepper to taste, and stir-fry for 5 minutes. Pour over the wine and let it bubble, then cover and simmer for 10 minutes.

VARIATION

Use penne instead of the farfalle, and asparagus tips instead of the courgettes.

2 Cook the pasta in a saucepan of salted boiling water according to the instructions on the packet. Meanwhile, add the crème fraîche to the courgette mixture and simmer for about 10 minutes until well reduced.

3 Add the prawns to the courgette mixture, heat through gently and taste for seasoning. Drain the pasta and tip it into a warmed bowl. Add the sauce and chopped herbs and toss well. Serve immediately.

Penne ai Gamberetti con Pernod

Penne with Prawns and Pernod

THIS IS A MODERN RECIPE, typical of those found on menus in the most innovative Italian restaurants. The Pernod and dill go well together, but you could use white wine and basil.

INGREDIENTS

200ml/7fl oz/scant 1 cup panna da cucina
 or double cream
250ml/8fl oz/1 cup fish stock
350g/12oz/3 cups dried penne
30–45ml/2–3 tbsp Pernod
225g/8oz/1⅓ cups peeled cooked prawns,
 thawed and thoroughly dried if frozen
30ml/2 tbsp chopped fresh dill, plus extra
 to garnish
salt and ground black pepper
Serves 4

1 Put the cream and the fish stock in a medium saucepan and bring to the boil. Lower the heat and simmer, stirring occasionally, for 10–15 minutes until reduced by about half. Meanwhile, cook the dried pasta in a saucepan of salted boiling water according to the instructions on the packet.

2 Add the Pernod and prawns to the cream sauce, with salt and pepper to taste, if necessary. Heat the prawns through very gently. Drain the pasta and tip it into a warmed bowl. Pour the sauce over the pasta, add the dill and toss well. Serve immediately, sprinkled with chopped dill.

Pizzoccheri della Valtellina

Buckwheat Noodles with Cabbage, Potatoes and Cheese

THIS IS A VERY UNUSUAL PASTA dish from Valtellina in the Italian Alps. The buckwheat noodles are unique to this area, and the dish takes its name from them.

INGREDIENTS

400g/14oz Savoy cabbage, cut into
    1cm/1/2in strips
2 potatoes, total weight about 200g/7oz,
    cut into 5mm/1/4in slices
400g/14oz dried pizzoccheri
75g/3oz/6 tbsp butter
1 generous bunch fresh sage
    leaves, shredded
2 garlic cloves
200g/7oz Fontina cheese, rind removed and
    thinly sliced
30–45ml/2–3 tbsp freshly grated
    Parmesan cheese, plus extra to serve
salt and ground black pepper
Serves 6

1 Bring a very large saucepan of salted water to the boil. Add the cabbage and potatoes and boil for 5 minutes.

2 Add the pasta, stir well and let the water return to the boil. Lower the heat and simmer for 15 minutes, or according to the instructions on the packet, until the pasta is *al dente*.

3 A few minutes before the pasta is ready, melt the butter in a small saucepan. Add the sage and whole garlic cloves and fry over a low to medium heat until the garlic is golden and sizzling. Lift the garlic out of the pan and discard it. Set the sage and garlic butter aside.

4 Drain the pasta and vegetables. Pour a quarter of the mixture into a warmed large bowl and arrange about a third of the Fontina slices on top. Repeat these layers until all the ingredients have been used, then sprinkle with the grated Parmesan. Pour the sage and garlic butter over the top and serve immediately, with extra Parmesan handed separately.

COOK'S TIPS

• Look for packets of dried pizzoccheri pasta in Italian delicatessens.
• Fontina is a mountain cheese with a sweet, nutty taste that is quite widely available, but if you cannot get it, look for Taleggio, Gruyère or Emmental – they are all similar cheeses. Cooks in the mountain regions of northern Italy would probably use either bitto or casera cheese, but these are not so easy to obtain outside the region.
• When in season, Swiss chard is used instead of cabbage, as is spinach.

Fettuccine al Burro e Parmigiano

Fettuccine with Butter and Parmesan

VERY FEW INGREDIENTS are needed to make up this incredibly simple dish. It comes from northern Italy, where butter and cheese are the most popular ingredients for serving with pasta. Children love it.

INGREDIENTS

400g/14oz fresh or dried fettuccine
50g/2oz/1/4 cup unsalted butter, cubed
115g/4oz/1 1/3 cups freshly grated
    Parmesan cheese
salt and ground black pepper
Serves 4

1 Cook the pasta in a pan of salted boiling water according to the instructions on the packet. Drain thoroughly, then tip into a warmed bowl.

2 Add the butter and Parmesan a third at a time, tossing the pasta after each addition until it is evenly coated. Season to taste and serve.

Vermicelli al Limone

Vermicelli with Lemon

FRESH AND TANGY, THIS MAKES an excellent first course for a dinner party. It doesn't rely on fresh seasonal ingredients, so it is good at any time of year. It is also a recipe to remember when you're pushed for time, because the sauce can easily be made in the time it takes to cook the pasta.

INGREDIENTS
350g/12oz dried vermicelli
juice of 2 large lemons
50g/2oz/¹/4 cup butter
200ml/7fl oz/scant 1 cup panna da cucina
  or double cream
115g/4oz/1¹/3 cups freshly grated
  Parmesan cheese
salt and ground black pepper
Serves 4

1 Cook the pasta in salted boiling water according to the instructions on the packet.

2 Meanwhile, pour the lemon juice into a medium saucepan. Add the butter and cream, then salt and pepper to taste.

3 Bring to the boil, then lower the heat and simmer for about 5 minutes, stirring occasionally, until the cream reduces slightly.

4 Drain the pasta and return it to the pan. Add the grated Parmesan, then taste the sauce for seasoning and pour it over the pasta. Toss quickly over a medium heat until the pasta is evenly coated with the sauce, then divide among four warmed bowls and serve immediately.

COOK'S TIP

Lemons vary in the amount of juice they yield. On average, a large fresh lemon will yield 60–90ml/4–6 tbsp. The lemony flavour of this dish is quite sharp – you can use less juice if you prefer.

VARIATIONS

• *Use spaghettini or spaghetti, or even small pasta shapes, such as fusilli, farfalle or orecchiette.*
• *For an even tangier taste, add a little grated lemon rind to the sauce when you add the butter and the cream to the pan in Step 2.*

Spaghetti allo Zafferano
Spaghetti with Saffron

A QUICK AND EASY DISH THAT makes a delicious midweek supper. The ingredients are all staples that you are likely to have in the fridge, so this recipe is perfect for impromptu meals.

INGREDIENTS

350g/12oz dried spaghetti
a few saffron strands
30ml/2 tbsp water
150g/5oz cooked ham, cut into thin strips
200ml/7fl oz/scant 1 cup panna da cucina
    or double cream
50g/2oz/²/₃ cup freshly grated Parmesan
    cheese, plus extra to serve
2 egg yolks
salt and ground black pepper
Serves 4

3 Add the strips of ham to the pan containing the saffron. Stir in the cream and Parmesan, with a little salt and pepper to taste. Heat gently, stirring all the time. When the cream starts to bubble around the edges, remove the sauce from the heat and add the egg yolks. Beat well to mix, then taste for seasoning.

4 Drain the pasta and tip it into a warmed bowl. Immediately pour the sauce over the pasta and toss well. Serve immediately, with extra grated Parmesan handed separately.

COOK'S TIPS

• Individual sachets of saffron powder, enough for four servings, are sold at Italian delicatessens and some supermarkets, and one sachet can be used for this sauce instead of the saffron strands. Simply sprinkle in the powder in Step 3, when adding salt and pepper.
• Use a heavy-based pan for heating the cream so that it does not catch on the bottom. Make sure you beat the sauce immediately the eggs are added.

1 Cook the pasta in a saucepan of salted boiling water according to the instructions on the packet.

2 Meanwhile, put the saffron strands in a saucepan, add the water and bring to the boil immediately. Remove the pan from the heat and leave to stand for a while.

Chiaroscuro

Black Pasta with Ricotta

THIS IS DESIGNER PASTA at its most dramatic, the kind of dish you are most likely to see at a fashionable Italian restaurant. Serve it for a smart dinner party first course – it will be a great talking point.

INGREDIENTS

300g/11oz dried black pasta
60ml/4 tbsp ricotta cheese, as fresh
   as possible
60ml/4 tbsp extra virgin olive oil
1 small fresh red chilli, seeded and
   finely chopped
1 small handful fresh basil leaves
salt and ground black pepper
Serves 4

1 Cook the pasta in salted boiling water according to the instructions on the packet. Meanwhile, put the ricotta in a bowl, add salt and pepper to taste and use a little of the hot water from the pasta pan to mix it to a smooth, creamy consistency. Taste for seasoning.

2 Drain the pasta. Heat the oil gently in the clean pan and add the pasta with the chilli and salt and pepper to taste. Toss quickly over a high heat to combine.

3 Divide the pasta equally among four warmed bowls, then top with the ricotta. Sprinkle with the basil leaves and serve immediately. Each diner tosses their own portion of pasta and cheese.

COOK'S TIP

Black pasta is made with squid ink. If you prefer, use green spinach-flavoured pasta or red tomato-flavoured pasta.

Paglia e Fieno alle Noci e Gorgonzola

Paglia e Fieno with Walnuts and Gorgonzola

CHEESE AND NUTS ARE popular ingredients for pasta sauces. The combination is very rich, so reserve this dish for a dinner party starter. It needs no accompaniment other than wine – a dry white would be good.

INGREDIENTS

275g/10oz dried paglia e fieno
25g/1oz/2 tbsp butter
5ml/1 tsp finely chopped fresh sage or
   2.5ml/1/2 tsp dried sage, plus fresh sage
   leaves, to garnish (optional)
115g/4oz torta di Gorgonzola
   cheese, diced
45ml/3 tbsp mascarpone cheese
75ml/5 tbsp milk
50g/2oz/1/2 cup walnut halves, ground
30ml/2 tbsp freshly grated Parmesan cheese
freshly ground black pepper
Serves 4

1 Cook the pasta in a large saucepan of salted boiling water, according to the instructions on the packet. Meanwhile, melt the butter in a large skillet or saucepan over a low heat, add the sage and stir it around. Sprinkle in the diced *torta di Gorgonzola* and then add the mascarpone. Stir the ingredients with a wooden spoon until the cheeses start to melt. Pour in the milk and keep stirring.

2 Sprinkle in the walnuts and grated Parmesan and add plenty of black pepper. Continue to stir over a low heat until the mixture forms a creamy sauce. Do not allow it to boil or the nuts will taste bitter, and do not cook the sauce for longer than a few minutes or the nuts will discolour it.

3 Drain the pasta, tip it into a warmed bowl, then add the sauce and toss well. Serve immediately, with more black pepper ground on top. Garnish with sage leaves, if you wish.

COOK'S TIP

Ready-ground nuts are sold in packets in supermarkets, but you will get a better flavour if you buy walnut halves and grind them yourself in a food processor.

Garganelli agli Asparagi e Panna

Garganelli with Asparagus and Cream

A LOVELY RECIPE FOR LATE spring when bunches of fresh young asparagus are on sale in shops and markets everywhere.

INGREDIENTS

1 bunch fresh young asparagus,
 250–300g/9–11oz
350g/12oz/3 cups dried garganelli
25g/1oz/2 tbsp butter
200ml/7fl oz/scant 1 cup panna da cucina
 or double cream
30ml/2 tbsp dry white wine
90–115g/3½–4oz/1–1⅓ cups freshly
 grated Parmesan cheese
30ml/2 tbsp chopped fresh mixed herbs,
 such as basil, flat leaf parsley, chervil,
 marjoram and oregano
salt and ground black pepper

Serves 4

3 Cook the pasta according to the instructions on the packet. Meanwhile, put the butter and cream in a medium saucepan, add salt and pepper to taste and bring to the boil. Simmer for a few minutes until the cream reduces and thickens, then add the asparagus, wine and about half the grated Parmesan. Taste for seasoning and keep on a low heat.

4 Drain the pasta when cooked and tip it into a warmed bowl. Pour the sauce over the pasta, sprinkle with the fresh herbs and toss well. Serve immediately, topped with the remaining grated Parmesan.

COOK'S TIPS

• *When buying asparagus look for thin stalks, which will be sweet and tender. Don't buy asparagus with thick or woody stalks, which will be tough.*

• *Garganelli all'uovo (with egg) are just perfect for this dish. You can buy packets of this pasta in Italian delicatessens.*

• *Penne (quills) or penne rigate (ridged quills) are an alternative pasta for this recipe. They are similar in shape and size to garganelli.*

1 Trim off and throw away the woody ends of the asparagus – after trimming, you should have about 200g/7oz asparagus spears. Cut the spears diagonally into pieces that are roughly the same length and shape as the garganelli.

2 Blanch the asparagus spears in salted boiling water for 2 minutes, the tips for 1 minute. Immediately after blanching drain the asparagus spears and tips, rinse in cold water and set aside.

Tagliatelle al Radicchio con Panna

Tagliatelle with Radicchio and Cream

3 Add the butter, onion and garlic to the pan and stir-fry for 5 minutes more. Add the radicchio and toss for 1–2 minutes until wilted.

4 Pour in the cream and add the grated Parmesan, with salt and pepper to taste. Stir for 1–2 minutes until the cream is bubbling and the ingredients are evenly mixed. Taste the sauce for seasoning.

THIS IS A MODERN RECIPE that is very quick and easy to make. It is deliciously rich, and makes a good dinner party first course.

INGREDIENTS

225g/8oz dried tagliatelle
75–90g/3–3¹/₂oz pancetta or rindless streaky bacon, diced
25g/1oz/2 tbsp butter
1 onion, finely chopped
1 garlic clove, crushed
1 head of radicchio, about 115–175g/4–6oz, finely shredded
150ml/¹/4 pint/²/₃ cup panna da cucina or double cream
50g/2oz/²/₃ cup freshly grated Parmesan cheese
salt and ground black pepper

Serves 4

1 Cook the pasta according to the instructions on the packet.

2 Meanwhile, put the pancetta or bacon in a medium saucepan and heat gently until the fat runs. Increase the heat slightly and stir-fry the pancetta or bacon for 5 minutes.

5 Drain the pasta and tip it into a warmed bowl. Pour the sauce over and toss well. Serve immediately.

COOK'S TIP

In Italy, cooks use a type of radicchio called radicchio di Treviso. It is very striking to look at, having long leaves that are dramatically striped in dark red and white. Radicchio di Treviso is available in some supermarkets and specialist greengrocers, but if you cannot get it you can use the round radicchio instead, which is very easy to obtain.

Vegetable Sauces

Pasta really comes into its own when it is served with a vegetable sauce. After all, when pasta was first "invented" it was a food for the poor, and vegetables were often all they could afford.

Vegetable sauces are invariably simple, in fact the simpler the better. Modern recipes often consist of nothing more elaborate than chopped or sliced raw vegetables "cooked" by the heat of freshly drained pasta. Colour, crunch and flavour are all retained, along with maximum nutritive value. Almost all the recipes in this chapter can be cooked in a very short time, making them perfect for quick after-work suppers. Some are made from only the barest ingredients and simply consist of fresh herbs, garlic and olive oil. These are the easiest of all pasta sauces to make, and some of the best.

Traditional vegetable sauces come from the south of Italy, where commercially dried pasta is favoured more than fresh. Generally speaking, dried pasta does seem to be the best choice for serving with vegetables, but for extra nutritional value there is no reason why fresh, egg-enriched pasta cannot be used.

Trenette alla Genovese

Trenette with Pesto, French Beans and Potatoes

IN LIGURIA, IT IS TRADITIONAL to serve pesto with trenette, French beans and diced potatoes. The ingredients for making fresh pesto are quite expensive, so the French beans and potatoes are added to help make the pesto go further.

INGREDIENTS

about 40 fresh basil leaves
2 garlic cloves, thinly sliced
25ml/1 1/2 tbsp pine nuts
45ml/3 tbsp freshly grated Parmesan
* cheese, plus extra to serve*
30ml/2 tbsp freshly grated Pecorino cheese,
* plus extra to serve*
60ml/4 tbsp extra virgin olive oil
2 potatoes, total weight about 250g/9oz
100g/3 1/2oz French beans
350g/12oz dried trenette
salt and ground black pepper
Serves 4

1 Put the basil leaves, garlic, pine nuts and cheeses in a blender or food processor and process for about 5 seconds. Add half the olive oil and a pinch of salt and process for 5 seconds more. Stop the machine, remove the lid and scrape down the side of the bowl. Add the remaining oil and process for 5–10 seconds.

2 Cut the potatoes in half lengthways. Slice each half crossways into 5mm/1/4in thick slices. Top and tail the beans, then cut them into 2cm/3/4in pieces. Plunge the potatoes and beans into a large saucepan of salted boiling water and boil, uncovered, for 5 minutes.

3 Add the pasta, bring the water back to the boil, stir well, then cook for 5–7 minutes or until the pasta is *al dente*.

4 Meanwhile, put the pesto in a large bowl and add 45–60ml/ 3–4 tbsp of the water used for cooking the pasta. Mix well.

5 Drain the pasta and vegetables, add them to the pesto and toss well. Serve immediately on warmed plates, with extra grated Parmesan and Pecorino handed separately.

COOK'S TIPS

• *Don't worry if the potatoes break up during cooking – this will add to the creaminess of the finished dish.*
• *The pesto can be made up to 2–3 days in advance and kept in a bowl in the fridge until needed. Pour a thin film of olive oil over the surface of the pesto and cover the bowl tightly with clear film before refrigerating.*
• *Trenette is the traditional Ligurian pasta that is served with pesto, but if you find it difficult to obtain you can use bavette or linguine instead. The two-coloured paglia e fieno would be another good choice.*

Paglia e Fieno con Pomodori Secchi e Radicchio

Paglia e Fieno with Sun-dried Tomatoes and Radicchio

THIS IS A LIGHT, MODERN PASTA dish of the kind served in fashionable restaurants. It is the presentation that sets it apart, not the preparation, which is very quick and easy.

INGREDIENTS

45ml/3 tbsp pine nuts
350g/12oz dried paglia e fieno
45ml/3 tbsp extra virgin olive oil
30ml/2 tbsp sun-dried tomato paste
2 pieces drained sun-dried tomatoes in olive oil, cut into very thin slivers
40g/1½oz radicchio leaves, finely shredded
4–6 spring onions, thinly sliced into rings
salt and ground black pepper
Serves 4

1 Put the pine nuts in a non-stick frying pan and toss over a low to medium heat for 1–2 minutes or until they are lightly toasted and golden. Remove and set aside.

2 Cook the pasta according to the packet instructions, keeping the colours separate by using two pans.

3 While the pasta is cooking, heat 15ml/1 tbsp of the oil in a medium skillet or saucepan. Add the sun-dried tomato paste and the sun-dried tomatoes, then stir in 2 ladlefuls of the water used for cooking the pasta. Simmer until the sauce is slightly reduced, stirring constantly.

4 Mix in the shredded radicchio, then taste and season if necessary. Keep on a low heat. Drain the paglia e fieno, keeping the colours separate, and return the noodles to the pans in which they were cooked. Add about 15ml/1 tbsp oil to each pan and toss over a medium to high heat until the pasta is glistening with the oil.

5 Arrange a portion of green and white pasta in each of four warmed bowls, then spoon the sun-dried tomato and radicchio mixture in the centre. Sprinkle the spring onions and toasted pine nuts decoratively over the top and serve immediately. Before eating, each diner should toss the sauce ingredients with the pasta to mix well.

COOK'S TIP

If you find the presentation too fiddly, you can toss the sun-dried tomato and radicchio mixture with the pasta in one large warmed bowl before serving, then serve it sprinkled with the spring onions and toasted pine nuts.

Penne con Salsa di Carciofi

Penne with Artichokes

ARTICHOKES ARE A VERY popular vegetable in Italy, and are often used in sauces for pasta. This sauce is garlicky and richly flavoured, the perfect dinner party first course during the globe artichoke season.

INGREDIENTS

juice of ¹/₂–1 lemon

2 globe artichokes

30ml/2 tbsp olive oil

1 small fennel bulb, thinly sliced, with feathery tops reserved

1 onion, finely chopped

4 garlic cloves, finely chopped

1 handful fresh flat leaf parsley, roughly chopped

400g/14oz can chopped Italian plum tomatoes

150ml/¹/₄ pint/²/₃ cup dry white wine

350g/12oz/3 cups dried penne

10ml/2 tsp capers, chopped

salt and ground black pepper

freshly grated Parmesan cheese, to serve

Serves 6

1 Have ready a bowl of cold water to which you have added the juice of half a lemon. Cut off the artichoke stalks, then discard the outer leaves until the pale inner leaves that are almost white at the base remain.

2 Cut off the tops of these leaves so that the base remains. Cut the base in half lengthways, then prise the hairy choke out of the centre with the tip of the knife and discard. Cut the artichokes lengthways into 5mm/¹/₄in slices, adding them immediately to the bowl of acidulated water.

3 Bring a large saucepan of water to the boil. Add a good pinch of salt, then drain the artichokes and add them immediately to the water. Boil for 5 minutes, drain and set aside.

4 Heat the oil in a large skillet or saucepan and add the fennel, onion, garlic and parsley. Cook over a low to medium heat, stirring frequently, for about 10 minutes until the fennel has softened and is lightly coloured.

5 Add the tomatoes and wine, with salt and pepper to taste. Bring to the boil, stirring, then lower the heat, cover the pan and simmer for 10–15 minutes. Stir in the artichokes, replace the lid and simmer for 10 minutes more. Meanwhile, cook the pasta in salted boiling water according to the instructions on the packet.

6 Drain the pasta, reserving a little of the cooking water. Stir the capers into the sauce, then taste for seasoning and add the remaining lemon juice if you like.

7 Tip the pasta into a warmed large bowl, pour the sauce over and toss well to mix, adding a little of the reserved cooking water if you like a runnier sauce. Serve immediately, garnished with the reserved fennel fronds. Hand around a bowl of grated Parmesan separately.

Spaghetti alla Bellini

Spaghetti with Aubergines

THIS FAMOUS DISH IS NAMED after the Sicilian composer. You may also come across it called Spaghetti alla Norma, after Bellini's opera.

INGREDIENTS

60ml/4 tbsp olive oil

1 garlic clove, roughly chopped

450g/1lb ripe Italian plum tomatoes, peeled and chopped

vegetable oil for shallow frying

350g/12oz aubergines, diced small

400g/14oz fresh or dried spaghetti

1 handful fresh basil leaves, shredded

115g/4oz ricotta salata cheese, coarsely grated

salt and ground black pepper

Serves 4–6

1 Heat the olive oil, add the garlic and cook over a low heat, stirring constantly, for 1–2 minutes. Stir in the tomatoes, then add salt and pepper to taste. Cover and simmer for 20 minutes.

2 Meanwhile, pour oil into a deep frying pan to a depth of about 1cm/1/2in. Heat the oil until hot but not smoking, then fry the aubergine cubes in batches for 4–5 minutes until tender and lightly browned. Remove the aubergine with a slotted spoon and drain on kitchen paper.

3 Cook the pasta according to the instructions on the packet. Meanwhile, stir the fried aubergines into the tomato sauce and warm through. Taste for seasoning.

4 Drain the pasta and tip it into a warmed bowl. Add the sauce, with the shredded basil and a generous handful of the grated ricotta salata. Toss well and serve immediately, with the remaining ricotta sprinkled on top.

COOK'S TIP

Some cooks sprinkle aubergines with salt and leave them for 20–30 minutes. This is said to help remove any bitterness, but it is not necessary if the aubergines are young and fresh.

Spaghetti al Rancetto

Spaghetti with Tomatoes and Pancetta

THIS SAUCE COMES FROM **Spoleto** in Umbria. It is a fresh, light sauce in which the tomatoes are cooked for a short time, so it should only be made in summer when tomatoes have a good flavour.

INGREDIENTS

350g/12oz ripe Italian plum tomatoes

150g/5oz pancetta or rindless streaky bacon, diced

30ml/2 tbsp olive oil

1 onion, finely chopped

350g/12oz fresh or dried spaghetti

2–3 fresh marjoram sprigs, leaves stripped

salt and ground black pepper

freshly grated Pecorino cheese, to serve

shredded fresh basil, to garnish

Serves 4

With a sharp knife, cut a cross in the bottom (flower) end of each plum tomato. Bring a medium saucepan of water to the boil and remove from the heat. Plunge a few of the tomatoes into the water; leave for 30 seconds or so, then lift them out with a slotted spoon and set aside. Repeat with the remaining tomatoes, then peel off the skin and finely chop the flesh.

COOK'S TIP

Do try to find pancetta – bacon can be substituted but the sauce will not taste precisely the same. You can buy ready diced pancetta in packets in supermarkets. Alternatively, you can buy it thinly sliced, sometimes cut from a roll (arrotolata), and dice it yourself.

2 Put the pancetta or bacon in a medium saucepan with the oil. Stir over a low heat until the fat runs. Add the onion and stir to mix. Cook gently for about 10 minutes, stirring.

3 Add the tomatoes, with salt and pepper to taste. Stir well and cook, uncovered, for about 10 minutes. Meanwhile, cook the pasta according to the instructions on the packet.

4 Remove the sauce from the heat, stir in the marjoram and taste for seasoning. Drain the pasta and tip it into a warmed bowl. Pour the sauce over the pasta and toss well. Serve immediately, sprinkled with shredded basil. Hand around grated Pecorino.

Penne all'Arrabbiata
Penne with Tomato and Chilli Sauce

THIS IS ONE OF ROME'S most famous
pasta dishes – penne tossed in a
tomato sauce flavoured with chilli.
Literally translated, *arrabbiata* means
"enraged" or "furious" but in this
context it should be translated as
"fiery". Make the sauce as hot as you
like by adding more chillies to taste.

INGREDIENTS

25g/1oz dried porcini mushrooms
90g/3 1/2oz/7 tbsp butter
150g/5oz pancetta or rindless smoked
  streaky bacon, diced
1–2 dried red chillies, to taste
2 garlic cloves, crushed
8 ripe Italian plum tomatoes, peeled
  and chopped
a few fresh basil leaves, torn, plus extra
  to garnish
350g/12oz/3 cups fresh or dried penne
50g/2oz/2/3 cup freshly grated
  Parmesan cheese
25g/1oz/1/3 cup freshly grated
  Pecorino cheese
salt
Serves 4

1 Soak the dried mushrooms in warm
water to cover for 15–20 minutes.
Drain, then squeeze dry with your
hands. Finely chop the mushrooms.

2 Melt 50g/2oz/4 tbsp of the butter
in a medium saucepan or skillet.
Add the pancetta or bacon and stir-fry
over a medium heat until golden and
slightly crispy. Remove the pancetta
with a slotted spoon and set it aside.

3 Add the chopped mushrooms to
the pan and cook in the same
way. Remove and set aside with the
pancetta or bacon. Crumble 1 chilli
into the pan, add the garlic and cook,
stirring, for a few minutes until the
garlic turns golden.

4 Add the tomatoes and basil and
season with salt. Cook gently,
stirring occasionally, for 10–15 minutes.
Meanwhile, cook the penne in a pan of
salted boiling water, according to the
instructions on the packet.

5 Add the pancetta or bacon and
the mushrooms to the tomato
sauce. Taste for seasoning, adding more
chillies if you prefer a hotter flavour. If
the sauce is too dry, stir in a little of the
pasta water.

6 Drain the pasta and tip it into a
warmed bowl. Dice the remaining
butter, add it to the pasta with the
cheeses, then toss until well coated.
Pour the tomato sauce over the pasta,
toss well and serve immediately, with a
few basil leaves sprinkled on top.

Conchiglie con Verdure Arrostite

Conchiglie with Roasted Vegetables

NOTHING COULD BE SIMPLER — or more delicious — than tossing freshly cooked pasta with roasted vegetables. The flavour is superb.

INGREDIENTS

1 red pepper, seeded and cut into
   1cm/¹/₂in squares
1 yellow or orange pepper, seeded and cut
   into 1cm/¹/₂in squares
1 small aubergine, roughly diced
2 courgettes, roughly diced
75ml/5 tbsp extra virgin olive oil
15ml/1 tbsp chopped fresh
   flat leaf parsley
5ml/1 tsp dried oregano or marjoram
250g/9oz baby Italian plum tomatoes,
   hulled and halved lengthways
2 garlic cloves, roughly chopped
350–400g/12–14oz/3–3¹/₂ cups dried
   conchiglie
salt and ground black pepper
4–6 fresh marjoram or oregano flowers,
   to garnish
Serves 4–6

1 Preheat the oven to 190°C/375°F/ Gas 5. Rinse the prepared peppers, aubergine and courgettes in a sieve or colander under cold running water, drain, then tip the vegetables into a large roasting tin.

2 Pour 45ml/3 tbsp of the olive oil over the vegetables and sprinkle with the fresh and dried herbs. Add salt and pepper to taste and stir well. Roast for about 30 minutes, stirring two or three times.

3 Stir the halved tomatoes and chopped garlic into the vegetable mixture, then roast for 20 minutes more, stirring once or twice. Meanwhile, cook the pasta according to the instructions on the packet.

4 Drain the pasta and tip it into a warmed bowl. Add the roasted vegetables and the remaining oil and toss well. Serve the pasta and vegetables hot in warmed bowls, sprinkling each portion with a few herb flowers.

COOK'S TIP

Pasta and roasted vegetables are very good served cold, so if you have any of this dish left over, cover it tightly with clear film, chill in the fridge overnight and serve it the next day as a salad. It would also make a particularly good salad to take on a picnic.

Conchiglie di Pisa

Conchiglie from Pisa

NOTHING COULD BE MORE simple than hot pasta tossed with fresh ripe tomatoes, ricotta and sweet basil. Serve it on hot summer days – it is surprisingly cool and refreshing.

INGREDIENTS

350g/12oz/3 cups dried conchiglie
125g/4¹/₂oz/generous ¹/₂ cup
  ricotta cheese
6 ripe Italian plum tomatoes, diced
2 garlic cloves, crushed
1 handful fresh basil leaves, shredded, plus
  extra basil leaves to garnish
60ml/4 tbsp extra virgin olive oil
salt and ground black pepper
Serves 4–6

1 Cook the pasta in salted boiling water according to the instructions on the packet.

COOK'S TIP

If you like, peel the tomatoes before you dice them. It won't take long if the tomatoes are ripe.

2 Meanwhile, put the ricotta in a large bowl and mash with a fork.

3 Add the tomatoes, garlic and basil, with salt and pepper to taste, and mix well. Add the olive oil and whisk thoroughly. Taste for seasoning.

4 Drain the cooked pasta, tip it into the ricotta mixture and toss well to mix. Garnish with basil leaves and serve immediately.

VARIATIONS

• *You can use diced mozzarella instead of ricotta cheese and call the dish* Conchiglie Caprese, *after the salad of tomatoes, mozzarella and basil known as Caprese.*
• *An avocado is the ideal ingredient for adding extra colour and flavour to this pasta dish. Halve, stone and peel, then dice the flesh. Toss it with the hot pasta at the last minute.*

Tagliatelle alle Erbe

Tagliatelle with Herbs

THIS IS A LOVELY dish for summer when fresh herbs are plentiful. It is quick and ideal for vegetarians.

INGREDIENTS

3 rosemary sprigs
1 small handful fresh flat leaf parsley
5–6 fresh mint leaves
5–6 fresh sage leaves
8–10 large fresh basil leaves
30ml/2 tbsp extra virgin olive oil
50g/2oz/¼ cup butter
1 shallot, finely chopped
2 garlic cloves, finely chopped
pinch of chilli powder, to taste
400g/14oz fresh egg tagliatelle
1 bay leaf
120ml/4fl oz/½ cup dry white wine
90–120ml/6–8 tbsp vegetable stock
salt and ground black pepper
Serves 4

1 Strip the rosemary and parsley leaves from their stalks and chop them together with the fresh mint, sage and basil.

2 Heat the olive oil and half the butter in a large skillet or saucepan. Add the shallot and garlic and the chilli powder, and cook over a very low heat, stirring frequently, for 2–3 minutes.

3 Cook the pasta in salted boiling water according to the packet instructions.

4 Add the chopped herbs and the bay leaf to the shallot mixture and stir for 2–3 minutes, then add the wine and increase the heat. Boil rapidly for 1–2 minutes until the wine reduces. Lower the heat, add the stock and simmer gently for 1–2 minutes.

5 Drain the pasta and add it to the herb mixture. Toss well to mix and remove and discard the bay leaf.

6 Put the remaining butter in a warmed large bowl, tip the dressed pasta into it and toss well to mix. Serve immediately.

Garganelli Primavera

Garganelli with Spring Vegetables

YOUNG FRESH VEGETABLES both look and taste good with pasta. Butter is used to marry the two together, but you can use extra virgin olive oil if you prefer.

INGREDIENTS

1 bunch asparagus, about 350g/12oz
4 young carrots
1 bunch spring onions
130g/4½oz shelled fresh peas
350g/12oz/3 cups dried garganelli
60ml/4 tbsp dry white wine
75g/3oz/6 tbsp unsalted butter, diced
a few sprigs each fresh flat leaf parsley,
   mint and basil, leaves stripped
   and chopped
salt and ground black pepper
freshly grated Parmesan cheese, to serve
Serves 4

1 Trim off and discard the woody part of each asparagus stem, then cut off the tips on the diagonal. Cut the stems on the diagonal into 4cm/1½in pieces. Cut the carrots and spring onions on the diagonal into similar pieces.

2 Plunge the asparagus stems, carrots and peas into a saucepan of salted boiling water. Bring back to the boil and simmer for 5–8 minutes, adding the asparagus tips for the last 3 minutes.

3 Meanwhile, cook the pasta in salted boiling water according to the instructions on the packet.

4 Drain the vegetables and return them to the pan. Add the wine, butter and salt and pepper to taste, then toss over a medium to high heat until the wine has reduced and the vegetables glisten with melted butter.

5 Drain the pasta and tip it into a warmed large bowl. Add the vegetables, spring onions and herbs and toss well. Serve immediately, with freshly grated Parmesan.

COOK'S TIP

Garganelli are rolled short pasta shapes made with egg. If you can't get garganelli, use another short shape made with egg.

Spaghetti al Pesto di Rucola

Spaghetti with Rocket Pesto

THIS IS THE PESTO for real rocket lovers. It is sharp and peppery, and delicious for a summer pasta meal with a glass of chilled dry white wine.

INGREDIENTS

4 garlic cloves

90ml/6 tbsp pine nuts

2 large handfuls rocket, total weight about
    150g/5oz, stalks removed

50g/2oz/²/3 cup Parmesan cheese,
    freshly grated

50g/2oz/²/3 cup Pecorino cheese,
    freshly grated

90ml/6 tbsp extra virgin olive oil

400g/14oz fresh or dried spaghetti

salt and ground black pepper

freshly grated Parmesan and Pecorino cheese,
    to serve

Serves 4

1 Put the garlic and pine nuts in a blender or food processor and process until finely chopped.

2 Add the rocket, Parmesan and Pecorino, oil and salt and pepper to taste and process for 5 seconds. Stop and scrape down the side of the bowl. Process for 5–10 seconds more until a smooth paste is formed.

3 Cook the spaghetti in a saucepan of salted boiling water according to the packet instructions.

4 Turn the pesto into a large bowl. Just before the pasta is ready, add 1–2 ladlefuls of the cooking water to the pesto and stir well to mix.

5 Drain the pasta, tip it into the bowl of pesto and toss well to mix. Serve immediately, with the grated cheeses handed separately.

VARIATION

To temper the flavour of the rocket and make the pesto milder, add 115g/4oz/¹/2 cup ricotta or mascarpone cheese to the pesto in Step 4 and mix well before adding the water.

Farfalle al Sugo di Piselli
Farfalle with Tomatoes and Peas

THIS PRETTY SAUCE should be served with plain white pasta so that the red, green and white make it tricolore, the three colours of the Italian flag. Here farfalle (bow-tie shaped pasta) are used, but other pasta shapes will work just as well.

INGREDIENTS

15ml/1 tbsp olive oil
5–6 rindless streaky bacon rashers, cut
*   into strips*
400g/14oz can chopped Italian
*   plum tomatoes*
60ml/4 tbsp water
350g/12oz/3 cups dried farfalle
225g/8oz/2 cups frozen peas
50g/2oz/4 tbsp mascarpone cheese
a few fresh basil leaves, shredded
salt and ground black pepper
freshly grated Parmesan cheese,
*   to serve*
basil leaves, to garnish
Serves 4

1 Heat the oil in a medium saucepan and add the bacon. Cook over a low heat, stirring frequently, for 5–7 minutes.

2 Add the tomatoes and water, with salt and pepper to taste. Bring to the boil. Lower the heat, cover and simmer gently for about 15 minutes, stirring from time to time.

3 Meanwhile, cook the pasta in salted boiling water according to the instructions on the packet.

4 Add the peas to the tomato sauce, stir well to mix and bring to the boil. Cover the pan and cook for 5–8 minutes until the peas are cooked and the sauce is quite thick. Taste the sauce for seasoning.

5 Turn off the heat under the pan and add the mascarpone and shredded basil. Mix well, cover the pan and leave to stand for 1–2 minutes. Drain the pasta and tip it into a warmed bowl. Pour the sauce over the pasta and toss well. Serve immediately, garnished with basil, and hand round some grated Parmesan separately.

Tagliatelle Verdissime

Tagliatelle with Broccoli and Spinach

THIS IS AN EXCELLENT vegetarian supper dish. It is nutritious and filling, and needs no accompaniment. If you like, you can use tagliatelle flecked with herbs.

INGREDIENTS
2 heads of broccoli
450g/1lb fresh spinach,
   stalks removed
nutmeg
450g/1lb fresh or dried egg tagliatelle
about 45ml/3 tbsp extra virgin olive oil
juice of 1/2 lemon, or to taste
salt and ground black pepper
freshly grated Parmesan cheese,
   to serve
Serves 4

1 Put the broccoli in the basket of a steamer, cover and steam over boiling water for 10 minutes. Add the spinach to the broccoli, cover and steam for 4–5 minutes or until both are tender. Towards the end of the cooking time, sprinkle the vegetables with freshly grated nutmeg and salt and pepper to taste. Transfer the vegetables to a colander.

2 Add salt to the water in the steamer and fill the steamer pan with boiling water, then add the pasta and cook according to the instructions on the packet. Meanwhile, chop the broccoli and spinach in the colander.

3 Drain the pasta. Heat 45ml/3tbsp oil in the pasta pan, add the pasta and chopped vegetables and toss over a medium heat until evenly mixed. Sprinkle in the lemon juice and plenty of black pepper, then taste and add more lemon juice, oil, salt and nutmeg if you like. Serve immediately, sprinkled liberally with freshly grated Parmesan and black pepper.

VARIATIONS

• If you like, add a sprinkling of crushed dried chillies with the black pepper in Step 3.
• To add both texture and protein, garnish the finished dish with one or two handfuls of toasted pine nuts. They are often served with broccoli and spinach in Italy.

Eliche col Pesto

Eliche with Pesto

BOTTLED PESTO IS a useful stand-by, but if you have a food processor, it is very easy to make your own.

INGREDIENTS

50g/2oz/1 1/3 cups fresh basil leaves, plus
  fresh basil leaves, to garnish
2–4 garlic cloves
60ml/4 tbsp pine nuts
120ml/4fl oz/1/2 cup extra virgin olive oil
115g/4oz/1 1/3 cups freshly grated
  Parmesan cheese, plus extra to serve
25g/1oz/1/3 cup freshly grated
  Pecorino cheese
400g/14oz/3 1/2 cups dried eliche
salt and ground black pepper
Serves 4

1 Put the basil leaves, garlic and pine nuts in a blender or food processor. Add 60ml/4 tbsp of the olive oil. Process until the ingredients are finely chopped, then stop the machine, remove the lid and scrape down the sides of the bowl.

2 Turn the machine on again and slowly pour the remaining oil in a thin, steady stream through the feeder tube. You may need to stop the machine and scrape down the sides of the bowl once or twice to make sure everything is evenly mixed.

3 Scrape the mixture into a large bowl and beat in the cheeses with a wooden spoon. Taste and add salt and pepper if necessary.

4 Cook the pasta according to the instructions on the packet. Drain it well, then add it to the bowl of pesto and toss well. Serve immediately, garnished with the fresh basil leaves. Hand shaved Parmesan separately.

COOK'S TIP

Pesto can be made up to 2–3 days in advance. To store pesto, transfer it to a small bowl and pour a thin film of olive oil over the surface. Cover the bowl tightly with clear film and keep it in the fridge.

Pipe con Ricotta e Spinaci

Pipe with Ricotta, Saffron and Spinach

TOSSING PASTA IN RICOTTA is popular in Sicily and Sardinia, where this cheese is widely used in cooking. For best results, use fresh white ricotta, which is sold by weight in Italian delicatessens. Serve this fairly rich dish in small quantities. Omit the saffron, with its quite strong flavour, if liked.

INGREDIENTS

1 small pinch of saffron threads
300g/11oz/2³⁄4 cups dried pipe
300–350g/11–12oz fresh spinach,
  stalks removed
nutmeg
250g/9oz/generous 1 cup ricotta cheese
salt and ground black pepper
freshly grated Pecorino cheese, to serve
Serves 4–6

1 Soak the saffron threads in 60ml/4 tbsp warm water. Cook the pasta according to the packet instructions.

2 Meanwhile, wash the spinach and put the leaves in a saucepan with only the water clinging to the leaves. Season with freshly grated nutmeg, salt and pepper to taste,

3 Cover the pan and cook over a medium to high heat for about 5 minutes, shaking the pan occasionally, until the spinach is wilted and tender. Tip into a colander, press it to extract as much liquid as possible, then roughly chop it, letting the water drain through.

4 Put the ricotta in a large bowl. Strain in the saffron water. Add the spinach, beat well to mix, then add a ladleful or two of the pasta cooking water to loosen the mixture. Season.

5 Drain the pasta, reserving some of the cooking water. Add the pasta to the ricotta mixture and toss well, adding a little of the water if necessary. Serve at once, sprinkled with Pecorino.

Tagliarini al Tartufo Bianco

Tagliarini with White Truffle

THERE IS NOTHING QUITE like the fragrance and flavour of the Italian white truffle. It is one of the rarest and therefore most expensive of truffles, which comes from around the towns of Alba and Asti in Piedmont. This simple style of serving it is one of the best ways to enjoy it.

INGREDIENTS

350g/12oz fresh tagliarini
75g/3oz/6 tbsp unsalted butter, diced
60ml/4 tbsp freshly grated Parmesan cheese
nutmeg
1 small white truffle, about
  25–40g/1–1¹⁄2oz
salt and ground black pepper
Serves 4

1 Cook the pasta in salted boiling water according to the instructions on the packet.

2 Drain the cooked pasta thoroughly and tip it into a warmed large bowl. Add the diced butter, grated Parmesan, freshly grated nutmeg and a little salt and pepper to taste. Toss well until the pasta is coated in melted butter.

3 Divide the pasta equally among four warmed bowls and shave paper-thin slivers of the white truffle on top. Serve immediately.

COOK'S TIPS

• *White Italian truffles can be bought during the months of September and October from specialist food shops and delicatessens. They are very expensive, however, and there are some alternative ways of getting the flavour of truffles without the expense. Some Italian delicatessens sell "truffle cheese", which is a mountain cheese with shavings of truffle in it, and this can be used instead of the Parmesan and truffle in this recipe. Another alternative is to toss hot pasta in truffle oil and serve it with freshly grated Parmesan.*

• *In Piedmont a very thin home-made egg pasta called* tagliarin *or* tajarin *is used for this dish. Tagliarini are the nearest equivalent, or you could use* tagliatellini *or* tagliolini *instead, or even* fettuccine *if you like.*

Linguine con la Rucola

Linguine with Rocket

THIS IS A FIRST COURSE THAT you will find in many a fashionable restaurant in Italy. It is very quick and easy to make at home and is worth trying for yourself.

INGREDIENTS

350g/12oz fresh or dried linguine
120ml/4fl oz/½ cup extra virgin olive oil
1 large bunch rocket, about 150g/5oz,
*   stalks removed, shredded or torn*
75g/3oz/1 cup freshly grated
*   Parmesan cheese*
salt and ground black pepper
Serves 4

1 Cook the pasta in a large saucepan of salted boiling water according to the instructions on the packet, then drain thoroughly.

2 Heat about 60ml/4 tbsp of the olive oil in the pasta pan, then add the drained pasta, followed by the rocket. Toss over a medium to high heat for 1–2 minutes or until the rocket is just wilted, then remove the pan from the heat.

3 Tip the pasta and rocket into a warmed large bowl. Add half the freshly grated Parmesan and the remaining olive oil. Add a little salt and black pepper to taste.

4 Toss the mixture quickly to mix. Serve immediately, sprinkled with the remaining Parmesan.

COOK'S TIP

Buy rocket by the bunch from the green-grocer. The type sold in small cellophane packets in supermarkets is very expensive for this kind of dish. Always check when buying rocket that all the leaves are bright green. In hot weather, rocket leaves quickly turn yellow.

Spaghetti al Limone
Spaghetti with Lemon

THIS IS THE DISH TO MAKE when you get home and find there's nothing to eat. If you keep spaghetti and olive oil in the storecupboard and garlic and lemons in the vegetable rack, you can prepare the most delicious meal in minutes.

INGREDIENTS

350g/12oz dried spaghetti
90ml/6 tbsp extra virgin olive oil
juice of 1 large lemon
2 garlic cloves, cut into very thin slivers
salt and ground black pepper
freshly grated Parmesan cheese, to serve

Serves 4

1 Cook the pasta in a saucepan of salted boiling water according to the instructions on the packet, then drain well and return to the pan.

2 Pour the olive oil and lemon juice over the cooked pasta, sprinkle in the slivers of garlic and add salt and pepper to taste.

3 Toss the pasta over a medium to high heat for 1–2 minutes. Serve immediately in four warmed bowls, with freshly grated Parmesan.

COOK'S TIP

Spaghetti is the best type of pasta for this recipe, because the olive oil and lemon juice cling to its long thin strands – even more so if you serve it with freshly grated Parmesan. If you are out of spaghetti, use another dried long pasta shape instead, such as spaghettini, linguine or tagliatelle.

Spaghetti Aglio e Olio

Spaghetti with Garlic and Oil

IN ROME THEY RUN THE words together to pronounce the name of this dish as "spaghetti-ayo-e-oyo" or simply "ayo-e-oyo". Sometimes it is given its full name of *Spaghetti Aglio, Olio e Peperoncino* because chilli – *peperoncino* – is always included to give the dish some bite.

INGREDIENTS

400g/14oz fresh or dried spaghetti
90ml/6 tbsp extra virgin olive oil
2–4 garlic cloves, crushed
1 dried red chilli
1 small handful fresh flat leaf parsley,
  roughly chopped
salt
Serves 4

| Cook the pasta according to the packet instructions, adding plenty of salt to the water. (See Cook's Tips.)

2 Meanwhile, heat the oil very gently in a small frying pan or saucepan. Add the crushed garlic and whole dried chilli and stir over a low heat until the garlic is just beginning to brown. Remove the chilli and discard.

3 Drain the pasta and tip it into a warmed large bowl. Pour on the oil and garlic mixture, add the parsley and toss vigorously until the pasta glistens. Serve immediately.

COOK'S TIPS

• *Since the oil is such an important ingredient here, only use the very best cold-pressed extra virgin olive oil.*
• *Don't use salt in the oil and garlic mixture, because it will not dissolve sufficiently. This is why plenty of salt is recommended for cooking the pasta.*
• *In Rome, grated Parmesan is never served with Spaghetti Aglio e Olio, nor is the dish seasoned with pepper.*
• *In summer, Romans use fresh chillies, which they grow in pots on their terraces and window ledges.*

Sugo di Verdure
Green Vegetable Sauce

ALTHOUGH DESCRIBED AS *SUGO* in Italian, this is not a true sauce, because it does not have any liquid apart from the oil and melted butter. It is more a medley of vegetables. Tossed with freshly cooked pasta, it is ideal for a fresh and light lunch or supper. Allow about 450g/1lb dried pasta for this amount of sauce.

INGREDIENTS

2 carrots
1 courgette
75g/3oz French beans
1 small leek
1 handful fresh flat leaf parsley
2 ripe Italian plum tomatoes
25g/1oz/2 tbsp butter
45ml/3 tbsp extra virgin olive oil
2.5ml/1/2 tsp granulated sugar
115g/4oz/1 cup frozen peas
salt and ground black pepper
Serves 4

1 Dice the carrots and the courgette finely. Top and tail the French beans, then cut them into 2cm/3/4in lengths. Slice the leek thinly. Peel and dice the tomatoes. Chop the flat leaf parsley and set aside.

2 Melt the butter in the oil in a medium skillet or saucepan. When the mixture sizzles, add the prepared leek and carrots. Sprinkle the sugar over and fry, stirring frequently, for about 5 minutes.

3 Stir in the courgette, French beans, peas and plenty of salt and pepper. Cover and cook over a low to medium heat for 5–8 minutes until the vegetables are tender, stirring occasionally.

4 Stir in the parsley and chopped plum tomatoes and adjust the seasoning to taste. Serve at once, tossed with freshly cooked pasta of your choice.

Spaghettini all'Aglio Arrostito

Spaghettini with Roasted Garlic

ROASTED GARLIC TASTES sweet and is milder than you would expect.

INGREDIENTS

1 whole head of garlic
400g/14oz fresh or dried spaghettini
120ml/4fl oz/¹/₂ cup extra virgin olive oil
salt and ground black pepper
coarsely shaved Parmesan cheese, to serve
Serves 4

1 Preheat the oven to 180°C/350°F/ Gas 4. Place the garlic in an oiled baking tin and roast it for 30 minutes.

2 Cook the pasta in a saucepan of salted boiling water according to the instructions on the packet.

3 Leave the garlic to cool, then lay it on its side and slice off the top third with a sharp knife.

4 Hold the garlic over a bowl and dig out the flesh from each clove with the point of the knife. When all the flesh has been added to the bowl, pour in the oil and add plenty of black pepper. Mix well.

5 Drain the pasta and return it to the clean pan. Pour in the oil and garlic mixture and toss the pasta vigorously over a medium heat until all the strands are thoroughly coated. Serve immediately, with shavings of Parmesan handed separately.

VARIATION

For a fiery finish, sprinkle crushed, dried red chillies over the pasta when tossing it with the oil and garlic.

COOK'S TIP

Although you can now buy roasted garlic in supermarkets, it is best to roast it yourself for this simple recipe, so that it melts into the olive oil and coats the strands of pasta beautifully.

Pasta con Funghi
Pasta with Mushrooms

SERVED WITH WARM CIABATTA, this makes an excellent vegetarian supper dish.

INGREDIENTS

15g/1/2oz dried porcini mushrooms
175ml/6fl oz/3/4 cup warm water
45ml/3 tbsp olive oil
2 garlic cloves, finely chopped
1 handful fresh flat leaf parsley,
    roughly chopped
2 large pieces drained sun-dried tomato in
    olive oil, sliced into thin strips
120ml/4fl oz/1/2 cup dry white wine
225g/8oz/2 cups chestnut mushrooms,
    thinly sliced
475ml/16fl oz/2 cups vegetable stock
450g/1lb/4 cups dried short pasta shapes,
    e.g. ruote, penne, fusilli or eliche
salt and ground black pepper
rocket and/or fresh flat leaf parsley,
    to garnish

Serves 4

1 Put the dried porcini mushrooms in a bowl, pour the warm water over and leave to soak for 15–20 minutes. Tip into a fine sieve set over a bowl and squeeze the porcini with your hands to release as much liquid as possible. Reserve the strained soaking liquid. Chop the porcini finely.

2 Heat the oil and cook the garlic, parsley, sun-dried tomato strips and porcini over a low heat, stirring frequently, for about 5 minutes.

3 Stir in the wine, simmer for a few minutes until reduced, then stir in the chestnut mushrooms. Pour in the stock and simmer, uncovered, for 15–20 minutes more until the liquid has reduced and the sauce is quite thick and rich.

4 Cook the pasta according to the instructions on the packet.

5 Taste the mushroom sauce for seasoning. Drain the pasta, reserving a little of the cooking liquid, and tip it into a warmed large bowl. Add the mushroom sauce and toss well, thinning the sauce if necessary with some of the pasta cooking water. Serve immediately, sprinkled liberally with chopped rocket and/or parsley.

VARIATION

Fresh wild mushrooms can be used instead of chestnut mushrooms, but they are seasonal and often expensive. A cheaper alternative is to use a box of mixed wild mushrooms. These are sold in many supermarkets.

Spaghetti alla Puttanesca

Spaghetti with Tomatoes, Anchovies, Olives and Capers

FROM CAMPANIA IN THE SOUTH, this classic sauce has a strong flavour. *Alla puttanesca* means "prostitute style".

INGREDIENTS

30ml/2 tbsp olive oil
1 small onion, finely chopped
1 garlic clove, finely chopped
4 drained canned anchovies
50g/2oz/¹/2 cup pitted black olives, sliced
15ml/1 tbsp capers
400g/14oz can chopped Italian
  plum tomatoes
45ml/3 tbsp water
15ml/1 tbsp chopped fresh flat leaf parsley
350g/12oz fresh or dried spaghetti
salt and ground black pepper
Serves 4

1 Heat the oil in a medium saucepan and add the onion, garlic and drained anchovies. Cook over a low heat, stirring constantly, for 5–7 minutes or until the anchovies break down to form a very soft pulp. Add the black olives and capers and stir-fry for a minute or so.

2 Add the tomatoes, water, half the parsley and salt and pepper to taste. Stir well and bring to the boil, then lower the heat and cover the pan. Simmer gently for 30 minutes, stirring occasionally. Meanwhile, cook the pasta according to the packet instructions.

3 Drain the pasta and tip it into a warmed bowl. Taste the sauce for seasoning, pour it over the pasta and toss well. Serve immediately, with the remaining parsley sprinkled on top.

COOK'S TIP

Use good-quality, shiny black olives – Gaeta olives from Liguria are very good.

Bucatini all'Amatriciana

Bucatini with Tomato and Chilli Sauce

AMATRICIANA IS A CLASSIC tomato sauce named after the town of Amatrice in the Sabine hills, Lazio. If you visit Rome, you will see it on many restaurant menus served with either bucatini or spaghetti.

INGREDIENTS

15ml/1 tbsp olive oil
1 small onion, finely sliced
115g/4oz smoked pancetta or rindless
  smoked streaky bacon, diced
1 fresh red chilli, seeded and cut into
  thin strips
400g/14oz can chopped Italian
  plum tomatoes
30–45ml/2–3 tbsp dry white wine
  or water
350g/12oz dried bucatini
30–45ml/2–3 tbsp freshly grated Pecorino
  cheese, plus extra to serve (optional)
salt and ground black pepper
Serves 4

1 Heat the oil in a medium saucepan and cook the onion, pancetta and chilli over a low heat for 5–7 minutes, stirring. Add the tomatoes and wine or water, with salt and pepper to taste. Bring to the boil, stirring, then cover and simmer for 15–20 minutes, stirring occasionally. If the sauce is too dry, stir in a little of the pasta water.

2 Meanwhile, cook the pasta in a pan of salted boiling water according to the packet instructions.

3 Drain the pasta and tip it into a warmed bowl. Taste the sauce for seasoning, pour it over the pasta and add the grated Pecorino. Toss well. Serve immediately, with more grated Pecorino handed separately if liked.

COOK'S TIP

Always take care when dealing with chillies. They contain a substance called capsaicin, which will irritate delicate skin, so it's a good idea to wear rubber gloves.

Sugo Finto

Meaty Tomato Sauce

THE WORD FINTO means "mock" or "pretend", and this Roman sauce takes its name from the days when meat was scarce and expensive, so cooks would put a little meat fat in a tomato sauce to make it taste of meat. Sometimes meat stock was used for the same purpose.

INGREDIENTS

1 small onion
1 small carrot
2 celery sticks
2 garlic cloves
1 small handful fresh flat leaf parsley
50g/2oz ham or bacon fat, finely chopped
60–90ml/4–6 tbsp dry white wine, or more
  to taste
500g/1 1/4lb ripe Italian plum
  tomatoes, chopped
salt and ground black pepper
Serves 4

1 Chop the onion, carrot and celery finely in a food processor. Add the garlic cloves and parsley and process until finely chopped. Alternatively, chop everything by hand.

2 Put the chopped vegetable mixture in a medium shallow saucepan or skillet with the ham fat and cook, stirring, over a low heat for about 5 minutes. Add the wine, with salt and pepper to taste and simmer for 5 minutes, then stir in the tomatoes. Simmer for 40 minutes, stirring occasionally and adding a little hot water if the sauce seems too dry.

3 Have ready a large sieve placed over a large bowl. Carefully pour in the sauce and press it through the sieve with the back of a metal spoon, leaving behind the tomato skins and any tough pieces of vegetable that won't go through.

4 Return the sauce to the clean pan and heat it through, adding a little more wine or hot water if it is too thick. Taste the sauce for seasoning, then toss with hot, freshly cooked pasta of your choice.

COOK'S TIPS

• *Capelli d'angelo, preferably made without egg, is the traditional pasta to serve with* sugo finto, *but you can use tagliolini or tagliarini if you prefer.*
• *If you like, you can add about 7g/1/4oz dried porcini mushrooms, soaked, drained and squeezed dry, when first cooking the other vegetables.*

Maccheroni con i Broccoli in Tegame

Macaroni with Broccoli and Cauliflower

THIS IS A SOUTHERN ITALIAN DISH, full of flavour. Without the anchovies, it can be served to vegetarians.

INGREDIENTS

175g/6oz cauliflower florets, cut into
small sprigs
175g/6oz broccoli florets, cut into
small sprigs
350g/12oz/3 cups short-cut macaroni
45ml/3 tbsp extra virgin olive oil
1 onion, finely chopped
45ml/3 tbsp pine nuts
1 sachet of saffron powder, dissolved in
15ml/1 tbsp warm water
15–30ml/1–2 tbsp raisins, to taste
30ml/2 tbsp sun-dried tomato paste
4 bottled or canned anchovies in olive oil,
drained and chopped, plus extra
anchovies to serve (optional)
salt and ground black pepper
freshly grated Pecorino cheese,
to serve

Serves 4

1 Cook the cauliflower sprigs in a large saucepan of salted boiling water for 3 minutes. Add the broccoli and boil for another 2 minutes. Remove the vegetables from the pan with a large slotted spoon and set aside.

2 Add the pasta to the vegetable cooking water and bring the water back to the boil. Cook the pasta according to the instructions on the packet until it is *al dente*.

3 Meanwhile, heat the olive oil in a large skillet or saucepan, add the finely chopped onion and cook over a low to medium heat, stirring frequently, for 2–3 minutes or until golden. Add the pine nuts, the cooked broccoli and cauliflower, and the saffron water. Add the raisins, sun-dried tomato paste and a couple of ladlefuls of the pasta cooking water until the vegetable mixture has the consistency of a sauce. Finally, add plenty of pepper.

4 Stir well, cook for 1–2 minutes, then add the chopped anchovies. Drain the pasta and tip it into the vegetable mixture. Toss well, then taste for seasoning and add salt if necessary. Serve the pasta immediately in four warmed bowls, sprinkled with freshly grated Pecorino. If you like the flavour of anchovies, add 1–2 whole anchovies to each serving.

Cappelletti con Pomodoro e Panna

Cappelletti with Tomatoes and Cream

TOMATOES, CREAM AND FRESH BASIL are a winning combination. In this very quick and easy recipe, the sauce coats little pasta hats filled with soft cheeses to make a substantial supper dish for vegetarians. If you prefer a lighter dish, you can use the sauce to coat plain, unstuffed pasta. Small shapes such as penne, farfalle or conchiglie are best.

INGREDIENTS

400ml/14fl oz/1⅔ cups passata
90ml/6 tbsp dry white wine
150ml/¼ pint/⅔ cup double cream
225g/8oz/2½ cups fresh cappelletti
1 small handful of fresh basil leaves
60ml/4 tbsp freshly grated Parmesan cheese
salt and ground black pepper
Serves 4–6

1 Pour the passata and wine into a medium saucepan and stir to mix. Bring to the boil over a medium heat, then add the cream and stir until evenly mixed and bubbling. Turn the heat down to low and leave to simmer.

2 Cook the pasta until *al dente*: 5–7 minutes or according to the instructions on the packet. Meanwhile, finely shred most of the basil leaves and set aside with the whole leaves.

3 Drain the pasta well, return it to the pan and toss it with the grated Parmesan. Taste the sauce for seasoning, pour it over the pasta and toss well. Serve immediately, sprinkled with the shredded basil and whole basil leaves.

COOK'S TIPS

- *Cappelletti with a variey of fillings are available at supermarkets and Italian delicatessens.*
- *Other stuffed pasta shapes, such as tortelloni, ravioli, or the more unusual sacchettini (little purses), can be used with this sauce.*
- *The tomato sauce can be made up to a day ahead, then chilled until ready to use. Reheat gently in a heavy-based saucepan while the pasta is cooking.*

La Crudaiola

Raw Tomato Sauce

THIS IS A WONDERFULLY simple uncooked tomato sauce that goes well with many different kinds of pasta, both long strands and short shapes. It is always made in summer when plum tomatoes have ripened on the vine in the sun and have their fullest flavour.

INGREDIENTS

500g/1¼lb ripe Italian plum tomatoes
1 large handful fresh basil leaves
75ml/5 tbsp extra virgin olive oil
115g/4oz ricotta salata cheese, diced
1 garlic clove, crushed
salt and ground black pepper
coarsely shaved Pecorino cheese, to serve
Serves 4

1 Roughly chop the plum tomatoes, removing the cores and as many of the seeds as you can. Tear the basil leaves into shreds with your fingers.

2 Put all the ingredients (except the cheese) in a bowl, adding salt and pepper to taste, and stir well. Cover and leave at room temperature for 1–2 hours to let the flavours mingle.

3 Taste the sauce to check the seasoning before tossing it with hot, freshly cooked pasta of your choice. Serve immediately with shavings of Pecorino handed separately.

COOK'S TIPS

- *Ricotta salata is a salted and dried version of ricotta cheese. It is firmer than the traditional soft white ricotta, and can be easily diced, crumbled and even grated. It is available from some delicatessens. If you can't locate it, use feta cheese instead.*
- *Long pasta goes well with this sauce, especially bucatini or spaghetti, or you could serve it with short shapes, such as fusilli or orecchiette.*

Fish
and
Shellfish
Sauces

It is not surprising that seafood sauces are often served with pasta along the Italian coastline, and on the islands of Sicily and Sardinia, but they're very popular inland, too. Clams, mussels, tuna, prawns, anchovies, salmon, scallops and squid are the most common fish and shellfish used, but cooks in coastal areas also create unique pasta dishes using the local catch. These are hard to replicate elsewhere.

Sometimes seafood is cooked with tomatoes, sometimes with a cream-based sauce, so the look and taste of seafood pasta can vary considerably from one dish to another. Intense flavours are found in Sicilian recipes, such as *Spaghetti alla Siracusana* and *Spaghetti alla Bottarga*, while the popular modern classic *Penne, Panna e Salmone* is mild and creamy. *Spaghetti alla Caprese*, from the island of Capri, is fresh and light. Spaghetti is the traditional pasta to serve with seafood sauces, since so many of them are based on olive oil and tomatoes. It remains the all-time favourite, but other shapes work equally well. When partnered with seafood, pasta proves its versatility.

Spaghetti alle Vongole

Spaghetti with Clam Sauce

THIS IS ONE OF ITALY'S most famous pasta dishes, sometimes translated as "white clam sauce" to distinguish it from that other classic, clams in tomato sauce. It is how they serve clams with pasta in Venice.

INGREDIENTS

1kg/2¹/4lb fresh clams
60ml/4 tbsp olive oil
45ml/3 tbsp chopped fresh flat leaf parsley
120ml/4fl oz/¹/2 cup dry white wine
350g/12oz dried spaghetti
2 garlic cloves
salt and ground black pepper
Serves 4

1 Scrub the clams under cold running water, discarding any that are open or that do not close when sharply tapped against the work surface.

2 Heat half the oil in a large saucepan, add the clams and 15ml/1 tbsp of the parsley and cook over a high heat for a few seconds. Pour in the wine, then cover tightly. Cook for about 5 minutes, shaking the pan frequently, until the clams have opened. Meanwhile, cook the pasta in salted boiling water according to the instructions on the packet.

3 Using a slotted spoon, transfer the clams to a bowl, discarding any that have failed to open. Strain the liquid and set it aside. Put eight clams in their shells to one side for the garnish, then remove the rest from their shells.

4 Heat the remaining oil in the clean pan. Fry the whole garlic cloves over a medium heat until golden, crushing them with the back of a spoon. Remove the garlic with a slotted spoon and discard.

5 Add the shelled clams to the oil remaining in the pan, gradually add some of the strained liquid from the clams, then add plenty of pepper. Cook for 1–2 minutes, gradually adding more liquid as the sauce reduces. Add the remaining parsley and cook for 1–2 minutes.

6 Drain the pasta, add it to the pan and toss well. Serve in individual dishes, scooping the shelled clams from the bottom of the pan and placing some of them on top of each serving. Garnish with the reserved clams in their shells and serve immediately.

Penne ai Gamberi e Carciofi

Penne with Prawns and Artichokes

THIS IS A GOOD DISH TO MAKE in late spring or early summer, when greeny-purple baby artichokes appear in shops and on market stalls.

INGREDIENTS

juice of ¹/2 lemon
4 baby globe artichokes
90ml/6 tbsp olive oil
2 garlic cloves, crushed
30ml/2 tbsp chopped fresh mint
30ml/2 tbsp chopped fresh flat leaf parsley
350g/12oz/3 cups dried penne
8–12 peeled cooked king or tiger prawns,
  each cut into 2–3 pieces
25g/1oz/2 tbsp butter
salt and ground black pepper

Serves 4

1 Have ready a bowl of cold water to which you have added the lemon juice. To prepare the artichokes, cut off the artichoke stalks, if any, and cut across the tops of the leaves. Peel off and discard any tough or discoloured outer leaves.

2 Cut the artichokes lengthways into quarters and remove any hairy chokes from their centres. Finally, cut the pieces of artichoke lengthways into 5mm/¹/4in slices and put these in the bowl of acidulated water.

3 Drain the slices of artichoke and pat them dry. Heat the olive oil in a non-stick frying pan and add the artichokes, the crushed garlic and half the mint and parsley to the pan.

4 Season with plenty of salt and pepper. Cook over a low heat, stirring frequently, for about 10 minutes or until the artichokes feel tender when pierced with a sharp knife.

5 Meanwhile, cook the pasta in a large saucepan of salted boiling water according to the instructions on the packet.

6 Add the prawns to the artichokes, stir well to mix, then heat through gently for 1–2 minutes.

7 Drain the pasta and tip it into a warmed bowl. Add the butter and toss until it has melted. Spoon the artichoke mixture over the pasta and toss to combine. Serve immediately, sprinkled with the remaining herbs.

Pesce con Fregola

Fish with Fregola

THIS SARDINIAN SPECIALITY is a cross between a soup and a stew. Serve it with crusty Italian country bread to mop up the juices.

INGREDIENTS

75ml/5 tbsp olive oil

4 garlic cloves, finely chopped

1/2 small fresh red chilli, seeded and
  finely chopped

1 large handful fresh flat leaf parsley,
  roughly chopped

1 red snapper, about 450g/1lb, cleaned,
  with head and tail removed

1 red or grey mullet, about 500g/1 1/4 lb,
  cleaned, with head and tail removed

350–450g/12oz–1lb thick cod fillet

400g/14oz can chopped Italian
  plum tomatoes

175g/6oz/1 1/2 cups dried fregola

salt and ground black pepper

Serves 4–6

1 Heat 30ml/2 tbsp of the olive oil in a large flameproof casserole. Add the chopped garlic and chilli, with about half the chopped fresh parsley. Fry over a medium heat, stirring occasionally, for about 5 minutes.

2 Cut all of the fish into large chunks – including the skin and the bones in the case of the snapper and mullet – and add the pieces to the casserole as you cut them. Sprinkle the pieces with a further 30ml/2 tbsp of the olive oil and fry for a few minutes more.

3 Add the tomatoes, then fill the empty can with water and pour this into the pan. Bring to the boil. Stir in salt and pepper to taste, lower the heat and cook for 10 minutes, stirring occasionally.

4 Add the fregola and simmer for 5 minutes, then add 250ml/8fl oz/ 1 cup water and the remaining oil. Simmer for 15 minutes until the fregola is *al dente*.

5 If the sauce becomes too thick, add more water, then taste for seasoning. Serve hot, in warmed bowls, sprinkled with the remaining parsley.

COOK'S TIPS

• *You can make the basic fish sauce several hours in advance or even the day before, bringing it to the boil and adding ther fregola just before serving.*

• *Fregola is a tiny pasta shape from Sardinia. If you can't get it, use a tiny soup pasta (pastina), such as corallini or semi de melone.*

Conchiglie di Mare
Seafood Conchiglie

THIS IS A VERY SPECIAL MODERN dish, a warm salad composed of scallops, pasta and fresh rocket flavoured with roasted pepper, chilli and balsamic vinegar. It makes a substantial and impressive dinner party starter, or a main course for a light lunch.

INGREDIENTS

8 large fresh scallops
300g/11oz/2¾ cups dried conchiglie
15ml/1 tbsp olive oil
15g/½oz/1 tbsp butter
120ml/4fl oz/½ cup dry white wine
90g/3½oz rocket leaves, stalks trimmed
salt and ground black pepper

For the vinaigrette
60ml/4 tbsp extra virgin olive oil
15ml/1 tbsp balsamic vinegar
*1 piece bottled roasted pepper, drained and
    finely chopped*
1–2 fresh red chillies, seeded and chopped
1 garlic clove, crushed
5–10ml/1–2 tsp clear honey, to taste

Serves 4

1 Cut each scallop into 2–3 pieces. If the corals are attached, pull them off and cut each piece in half. Season the scallops and corals with salt and pepper.

2 To make the vinaigrette, put the oil, vinegar, chopped pepper and chillies in a jug with the garlic and honey and whisk well.

3 Cook the pasta according to the instructions on the packet.

4 Meanwhile, heat the oil and butter in a non-stick frying pan until sizzling. Add half the scallops and toss over a high heat for 2 minutes. Remove with a slotted spoon and keep warm. Cook the remaining scallops in the same way.

5 Add the wine to the liquid remaining in the pan and stir over a high heat until the mixture has reduced to a few tablespoons. Remove from the heat and keep warm.

6 Drain the pasta and tip it into a warmed bowl. Add the rocket, scallops, the reduced cooking juices and the vinaigrette and toss well to combine. Serve immediately.

COOK'S TIPS

• *Use only fresh scallops for this dish – they are available all year round in most fishmongers and from fish counters in supermarkets. Frozen scallops tend to be watery and tasteless, and often prove to be rubbery when cooked.*
• *For a more formal presentation, arrange the rocket leaves in a circle on each of four individual serving plates. Toss the pasta, scallops, reduced cooking juices and vinaigrette together and spoon into the centre of the rocket leaves.*

Spaghetti alla Siracusana
Spaghetti with Anchovies and Olives

THE STRONG FLAVOURS of this dish are typical of Sicilian cuisine.

INGREDIENTS
45ml/3 tbsp olive oil

1 large red pepper, seeded and chopped

1 small aubergine, finely chopped

1 onion, finely chopped

8 ripe Italian plum tomatoes, peeled, seeded
    and finely chopped

2 garlic cloves, finely chopped

120ml/4fl oz/¹/₂ cup dry red or white wine

120ml/4fl oz/¹/₂ cup water

1 handful fresh herbs, such as basil, flat leaf
    parsley and rosemary

300g/11oz dried spaghetti

50g/2oz canned anchovies, roughly chopped,
    plus extra whole anchovies to garnish

12 pitted black olives

15–30ml/1–2 tbsp capers, to taste

salt and ground black pepper

Serves 4

1 Heat the oil in a saucepan and add all the finely chopped vegetables and garlic. Cook gently, stirring frequently, for 10–15 minutes until the vegetables are soft. Pour in the wine and water, add the fresh herbs and pepper to taste and bring to the boil. Lower the heat and simmer, stirring occasionally, for 10–15 minutes. Meanwhile, cook the pasta in a large saucepan of salted boiling water according to the instructions on the packet.

2 Add the chopped anchovies, olives and capers to the sauce, heat through for a few minutes and taste for seasoning. Drain the pasta and tip it into a warmed bowl. Pour the sauce over the pasta, toss well and serve immediately.

COOK'S TIP

If the anchovies are omitted, this makes a good sauce for vegetarians.

Spaghetti alla Caprese
Spaghetti with Tuna, Anchovies, Olives and Mozzarella

THIS RECIPE FROM CAPRI is fresh, light and full of flavour, so serve it as soon as it is cooked to enjoy it at its best.

INGREDIENTS
300g/11oz dried spaghetti

30ml/2 tbsp olive oil

6 ripe Italian plum tomatoes, chopped

5ml/1 tsp granulated sugar

50g/2oz jar anchovies in olive oil, drained

about 60ml/4 tbsp dry white wine

200g/7oz can tuna in olive oil, drained

50g/2oz/¹/₂ cup pitted black olives,
    quartered lengthways

125g/4¹/₂oz packet mozzarella cheese,
    drained and diced

salt and ground black pepper

fresh basil leaves, to finish

Serves 4

1 Cook the pasta according to the instructions on the packet. Meanwhile, heat the oil in a medium saucepan. Add the tomatoes, sugar and pepper to taste, and toss over a medium heat for a few minutes until the tomatoes soften and the juices run. Snip a few anchovies at a time into the pan of tomatoes with kitchen scissors.

2 Add the wine, tuna and olives and stir once or twice until they are just evenly mixed into the sauce. Add the mozzarella and heat through without stirring. Taste and add salt if necessary. Drain the pasta and tip it into a warmed bowl. Pour the sauce over, toss gently and sprinkle with basil leaves. Serve immediately.

Orecchiette con Acciughe e Broccoli

Orecchiette with Anchovies and Broccoli

WITH ITS ROBUST FLAVOURS, this pasta dish is typical of southern Italian and Sicilian cooking. Anchovies, pine nuts, garlic and Pecorino cheese are all very popular ingredients. Serve with crusty Italian bread for a light lunch or supper.

INGREDIENTS

300g/11oz/2 cups broccoli florets
40g/1½oz/½ cup pine nuts
350g/12oz/3 cups dried orecchiette
60ml/4 tbsp olive oil
1 small red onion, thinly sliced
50g/2oz jar anchovies in olive oil
1 garlic clove, crushed
50g/2oz/⅔ cup freshly grated
  Pecorino cheese
salt and ground black pepper
Serves 4

COOK'S TIP

Orecchiette (little ears) from Puglia are a special type of pasta with a chewy texture. You can get them in Italian delicatessens, or use conchiglie instead.

1 Break the broccoli florets into small sprigs and cut off the stalks. If the stalks are large, chop or slice them. Cook the broccoli florets and stalks in a saucepan of boiling salted water for 2 minutes, then drain and refresh under cold running water. Leave to drain on kitchen paper.

2 Put the pine nuts in a dry non-stick frying pan and toss over a low to medium heat for 1–2 minutes or until the nuts are lightly toasted and golden. Remove and set aside.

3 Cook the pasta according to the instructions on the packet.

4 Meanwhile, heat the oil in a skillet, add the red onion and fry gently, stirring frequently, for about 5 minutes until softened. Add the anchovies with their oil, then add the garlic and fry over a medium heat, stirring frequently, for 1–2 minutes until the anchovies break down to form a paste. Add the broccoli and plenty of pepper and toss over the heat for a minute or two until the broccoli is hot. Taste for seasoning.

5 Drain the pasta and tip it into a warmed bowl. Add the broccoli mixture and grated Pecorino and toss well to combine. Sprinkle the pine nuts over the top and serve immediately.

Trenette ai Frutti di Mare

Trenette with Shellfish

COLOURFUL AND DELICIOUS, this typical Genoese dish is ideal for a dinner party. The sauce is quite runny, so serve it with crusty bread and spoons as well as forks.

INGREDIENTS

45ml/3 tbsp olive oil
1 small onion, finely chopped
1 garlic clove, crushed
1/2 fresh red chilli, seeded and chopped
200g/7oz can chopped Italian
 plum tomatoes
30ml/2 tbsp chopped fresh flat leaf parsley
400g/14oz fresh clams
400g/14oz fresh mussels
60ml/4 tbsp dry white wine
400g/14oz/3 1/2 cups dried trenette
a few fresh basil leaves
90g/3 1/2oz/2/3 cup peeled cooked prawns,
 thawed and thoroughly dried if frozen
salt and ground black pepper
chopped fresh herbs, to garnish
Serves 4

1 Heat 30ml/2 tbsp of the oil in a skillet or medium saucepan. Add the onion, garlic and chilli and cook over a medium heat for 1–2 minutes, stirring constantly. Stir in the tomatoes, half the parsley and pepper to taste. Bring to the boil, lower the heat, cover and simmer for 15 minutes.

2 Meanwhile, scrub the clams and mussels under cold running water. Discard any that are open or that do not close when sharply tapped against the work surface.

3 In a large saucepan, heat the remaining oil. Add the clams and mussels, with the rest of the parsley and toss over a high heat for a few seconds. Pour in the wine, then cover tightly. Cook for about 5 minutes, shaking the pan frequently, until the clams and mussels have opened.

4 Remove the pan from the heat and transfer the clams and mussels to a bowl with a slotted spoon, discarding any shellfish that have failed to open.

5 Strain the cooking liquid into a measuring jug and set aside. Reserve eight clams and four mussels in their shells for the garnish, then remove the rest from their shells.

6 Cook the pasta according to the instructions on the packet. Meanwhile, add 120ml/4fl oz/1/2 cup of the reserved seafood liquid to the tomato sauce. Bring to the boil over a high heat, stirring. Lower the heat, tear in the basil leaves and add the prawns with the shelled clams and mussels. Stir well, then taste for seasoning.

7 Drain the pasta and tip it into a warmed bowl. Add the seafood sauce and toss well to combine. Serve in individual bowls, sprinkle with herbs and garnish each portion with two reserved clams and one mussel in their shells.

Paglia e Fieno con Salsa di Gamberi e Vodka

Paglia e Fieno with Prawns and Vodka

THE COMBINATION OF PRAWNS, vodka and pasta may seem unusual, but it has become something of a modern classic in Italy. Here it is stylishly presented with two-coloured pasta, but the sauce goes equally well with short shapes such as penne, rigatoni and farfalle.

INGREDIENTS

30ml/2 tbsp olive oil
1/4 large onion, finely chopped
I garlic clove, crushed
15–30ml/1–2 tbsp sun-dried tomato paste
200ml/7fl oz/scant I cup panna da cucina or double cream
350g/12oz fresh or dried paglia e fieno
12 raw tiger prawns, peeled and chopped
30ml/2 tbsp vodka
salt and ground black pepper
Serves 4

1 Heat the oil in a medium saucepan, add the onion and garlic and cook gently, stirring frequently, for about 5 minutes until softened.

2 Add the tomato paste and stir for 1–2 minutes, then add the cream and bring to the boil, stirring. Season with salt and pepper to taste and let the sauce bubble until it starts to thicken slightly. Remove from the heat.

3 Cook the pasta according to the instructions on the packet. When it is almost ready, add the prawns and vodka to the sauce; toss quickly over a medium heat for 2–3 minutes until the prawns turn pink.

4 Drain the pasta and tip it into a warmed bowl. Pour the sauce over and toss well. Divide among warmed bowls and serve immediately.

COOK'S TIP

This sauce is best served as soon as it is ready, otherwise the prawns will overcook and become tough. Make sure that the pasta has only a minute or two of cooking time left before adding the prawns to the sauce.

Penne, Panna e Salmone

Penne with Cream and Smoked Salmon

THIS MODERN WAY OF serving pasta is popular all over Italy. The three essential ingredients combine together beautifully, and the dish is very quick and easy to make.

INGREDIENTS

350g/12oz/3 cups dried penne
115g/4oz thinly sliced smoked salmon
2–3 fresh thyme sprigs
25g/1oz/2 tbsp butter
150ml/1/4 pint/2/3 cup extra-thick single cream
salt and ground black pepper
Serves 4

1 Cook the pasta in a saucepan of salted boiling water according to the instructions on the packet.

2 Meanwhile, using kitchen scissors, cut the smoked salmon into thin strips, about 5mm/1/4in wide. Strip the leaves from the thyme sprigs.

3 Melt the butter in a large saucepan. Stir in the cream with about a quarter of the salmon and thyme leaves, then season with pepper. Heat gently for 3–4 minutes, stirring all the time. Do not allow to boil. Taste the sauce for seasoning.

4 Drain the pasta and toss it in the cream and salmon sauce. Divide among four warmed bowls and top with the remaining salmon and thyme leaves. Serve immediately.

VARIATION

Although penne is traditional with this sauce, it also goes very well with fresh ravioli stuffed with spinach and ricotta.

Spaghetti alla Bottarga

Spaghetti with Bottarga

ALTHOUGH THIS MAY SEEM an unusual recipe, with bottarga (salted and air-dried mullet or tuna roe) as the principal ingredient, it is very well known in Sardinia – and also in Sicily and parts of southern Italy. It is simplicity itself to make and tastes very, very good.

INGREDIENTS

350g/12oz fresh or dried spaghetti
about 60ml/4 tbsp olive oil
2–3 garlic cloves, peeled
ground black pepper
60–90ml/4–6 tbsp grated bottarga, to taste
Serves 4

1 Cook the pasta according to the instructions on the packet.

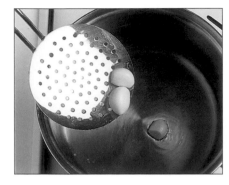

2 Meanwhile, heat half the olive oil in a large saucepan. Add the garlic and cook gently, stirring, for a few minutes. Remove the pan from the heat, scoop out the garlic with a slotted spoon and discard.

3 Drain the pasta very well. Return the pan of garlic-flavoured oil to the heat and add the pasta. Toss well, season with pepper and moisten with the remaining oil, or more to taste. Divide the pasta among four warmed bowls, sprinkle the grated bottarga over the top and serve immediately.

COOK'S TIP

You can buy bottarga in Italian delicatessens. Small jars of ready-grated bottarga are convenient, but the best flavour comes from vacuum-packed slices of mullet bottarga. This is very easy to grate on a box grater. Keep any leftover bottarga tightly wrapped in the fridge, so that it does not taint other foods.

Linguine al Granchio

Linguine with Crab

THIS RECIPE COMES FROM Rome. It makes a very rich and tasty first course on its own, or can be served for a lunch or supper with crusty Italian bread. Some cooks like a finer sauce, and work the crabmeat through a sieve after pounding. If you fancy following their example, be warned – it's hard work.

INGREDIENTS

about 250g/9oz shelled crabmeat
45ml/3 tbsp olive oil
1 small handful fresh flat leaf parsley,
*   roughly chopped, plus extra to garnish*
1 garlic clove, crushed
350g/12oz ripe Italian plum tomatoes,
*   skinned and chopped*
60–90ml/4–6 tbsp dry white wine
350g/12oz fresh or dried linguine
salt and ground black pepper

Serves 4

1 Put the crabmeat in a mortar and pound to a rough pulp with a pestle. If you do not have a pestle and mortar, use a sturdy bowl and the end of a rolling pin. Set aside.

2 Heat 30ml/2 tbsp of the oil in a large saucepan. Add the parsley and garlic, with salt and pepper to taste, and fry for a few minutes until the garlic begins to brown.

3 Add the tomatoes, pounded crabmeat and wine, cover the pan and simmer gently for 15 minutes, stirring occasionally.

4 Meanwhile, cook the pasta according to the instructions on the packet, draining it the moment it is *al dente*, and reserving a little of the cooking water.

5 Return the pasta to the clean pan, add the remaining oil and toss quickly over a medium heat until the oil coats the strands.

6 Add the tomato and crab mixture to the pasta and toss again, adding a little of the reserved cooking water if you think it necessary. Adjust the seasoning to taste. Serve hot, in warmed bowls, sprinkled with parsley.

COOK'S TIP

The best way to obtain crabmeat is to ask a fishmonger to remove it from the shell for you, or buy dressed crab from the supermarket. For this recipe you will need one large crab, and you should use both the white and dark meat.

Tagliatelle con Capesante

Tagliatelle with Scallops

SCALLOPS AND BRANDY MAKE this a relatively expensive dish, but it is so delicious that you will find it well worth the cost. Serve it for a dinner party first course.

INGREDIENTS

200g/7oz scallops, sliced
30ml/2 tbsp plain flour
40g/1 1/2oz/3 tbsp butter
2 spring onions, cut into thin rings
1/2–1 small fresh red chilli, seeded and very finely chopped
30ml/2 tbsp finely chopped fresh flat leaf parsley
60ml/4 tbsp brandy
105ml/7 tbsp fish stock
275g/10oz fresh spinach-flavoured tagliatelle
salt and ground black pepper

Serves 4

1 Toss the scallops in the flour, then shake off the excess. Bring a saucepan of salted water to the boil, ready for cooking the pasta.

2 Meanwhile, melt the butter in a skillet or large saucepan. Add the spring onions, finely chopped chilli and half the parsley and fry, stirring frequently, for 1–2 minutes over a medium heat. Add the scallops and toss over the heat for 1–2 minutes.

3 Pour the brandy over the scallops, then set it alight with a match. As soon as the flames have died down, stir in the fish stock and salt and pepper to taste. Mix well. Simmer for 2–3 minutes, then cover the pan and remove it from the heat.

4 Add the pasta to the boiling water and cook it according to the instructions on the packet. Drain, add to the sauce and toss over a medium heat until mixed. Serve at once, in warmed bowls sprinkled with the remaining parsley.

COOK'S TIP

Buy fresh scallops, with their corals if possible. Fresh scallops always have a better texture and flavour than frozen scallops, which tend to be watery.

Spaghetti con Seppie e Piselli

Spaghetti with Squid and Peas

IN TUSCANY, SQUID IS often cooked with peas in a tomato sauce. This recipe is a variation on the theme, and it works very well.

INGREDIENTS

450g/1lb prepared squid
30ml/2 tbsp olive oil
1 small onion, finely chopped
400g/14oz can chopped Italian plum tomatoes
1 garlic clove, finely chopped
15ml/1 tbsp red wine vinegar
5ml/1 tsp granulated sugar
10ml/2 tsp finely chopped fresh rosemary
115g/4oz/1 cup frozen peas
350g/12oz fresh or dried spaghetti
15ml/1 tbsp chopped fresh flat leaf parsley
salt and ground black pepper

Serves 4

1 Cut the prepared squid into strips about 5mm/1/4in wide. Finely chop any tentacles.

2 Heat the oil in a skillet or medium saucepan, add the finely chopped onion and cook gently, stirring, for about 5 minutes until softened. Add the squid, tomatoes, garlic, red wine vinegar and sugar.

3 Add the rosemary, with salt and pepper to taste. Bring to the boil, stirring, then cover and simmer gently for 20 minutes. Uncover the pan, add the peas and cook for 10 minutes. Meanwhile, cook the pasta according to the instructions on the packet, then drain and tip it into a warmed bowl. Pour the sauce over the pasta, add the parsley, then toss well and serve.

Spaghetti con Salmone e Gamberi

Spaghetti with Salmon and Prawns

THIS IS A LOVELY FRESH-TASTING pasta dish, perfect for an *al fresco* meal in summer. Serve it as a main course lunch with warm ciabatta or focaccia and a dry white wine.

INGREDIENTS

300g/11oz salmon fillet
200ml/7fl oz/scant 1 cup dry white wine
a few fresh basil sprigs, plus extra basil
    leaves, to garnish
6 ripe Italian plum tomatoes, peeled and
    finely chopped
150ml/¼ pint/⅔ cup double cream
350g/12oz/3 cups fresh or dried spaghetti
115g/4oz/⅔ cup peeled cooked prawns,
    thawed and thoroughly dried if frozen
salt and ground black pepper

Serves 4

1 Put the salmon skin-side up in a wide shallow pan. Pour the wine over, then add the basil sprigs to the pan and sprinkle the fish with salt and pepper. Bring the wine to the boil, cover the pan and simmer gently for no more than 5 minutes. Using a fish slice, lift the fish out of the pan and set aside to cool a little.

2 Add the cream and tomatoes to the liquid remaining in the pan and bring to the boil. Stir well, then lower the heat and simmer, uncovered, for 10–15 minutes. Meanwhile, cook the pasta according to the instructions on the packet.

3 Flake the fish into large chunks, discarding the skin and any bones. Add the fish to the sauce with the prawns, shaking the pan until the fish and shellfish are well coated. Taste the sauce for seasoning.

4 Drain the pasta and tip it into a warmed bowl. Pour the sauce over the pasta and toss to combine. Serve immediately, garnished with fresh basil leaves.

COOK'S TIP

Check the salmon fillet carefully for small bones when you are flaking the flesh. Although the salmon is already filleted, you will always find a few stray "pin" bones. Pick them out carefully using tweezers or your fingertips.

Spaghetti alla Carrettiera

Spaghetti with Tuna, Mushrooms and Bacon

THE TERM ALLA CARRETTIERA means "cart-driver's style". The Romans lay claim to this recipe, but so do the Neapolitans and Sicilians, so there are many different versions of it.

INGREDIENTS
15g/¹/₂oz dried porcini mushrooms
175ml/6fl oz/³/₄ cup warm water
30ml/2 tbsp olive oil
1 garlic clove
75g/3oz pancetta or rindless streaky bacon,
  cut into 5mm/¹/₄in strips
225g/8oz/3 cups button
  mushrooms, chopped
400g/14oz fresh or dried spaghetti
200g/7oz can tuna in olive oil, drained
salt and ground black pepper
freshly grated Parmesan cheese, to serve
Serves 4

1 Put the porcini in a small bowl. Pour over the warm water and leave to soak for 15–20 minutes.

2 Heat the oil in a large saucepan, add the garlic clove and cook gently for about 2 minutes, crushing it with a wooden spoon to release the flavour. Remove the garlic and discard. Add the pancetta or bacon to the oil remaining in the pan and cook for 3–4 minutes, stirring occasionally.

3 Meanwhile, drain the dried mushrooms, reserving the soaking liquid, and chop them finely.

4 Add both types of mushroom to the pan and cook, stirring, for 1–2 minutes, then add 90ml/6 tbsp of the reserved liquid from soaking the dried mushrooms, with salt and pepper to taste. Simmer for 10 minutes, stirring occasionally. Meanwhile, cook the pasta according to the instructions on the packet, adding the remaining soaking liquid from the mushrooms to the pasta cooking water.

5 Add the drained canned tuna to the mushroom sauce and fold it in gently. Taste for seasoning.

6 Drain the cooked pasta well and tip it into a warmed serving bowl. Pour the sauce over the top, toss well and sprinkle liberally with some freshly grated Parmesan. Serve immediately, with more Parmesan handed around separately.

Meat
and
Poultry
Sauces

When we think of a meat sauce to serve with pasta, our minds automatically turn to Bolognese sauce, or *ragù alla Bolognese*, as it is correctly called in Italian. Thanks to Italian emigrés, Bolognese sauce has become one of the most famous pasta sauces outside Italy, especially in Great Britain and the United States. Beef, pork and pancetta simmered with wine and tomatoes until rich, intensely meaty and satisfying, is very hard to beat. Unfortunately, this superb sauce is almost always served with spaghetti outside Italy, which is incorrect. It should be teamed with tagliatelle.

Many meat sauces hail from the north of Italy, especially from the region of Emilia-Romagna, where both fresh meat and the famous hams, salame and sausages are enjoyed in abundance. The actual quantity of meat in the sauce is never very large, however, and the size of the pieces must be small or the sauce will simply slide off the pasta. The egg-enriched pasta of the northern regions is good with meat sauces because it holds the sauce well, but it is by no means the only possibility. Long, thin types of pasta, such as spaghetti and vermicelli, find favour precisely because they do not hold a great deal of sauce, a point worth considering when a meat sauce is very rich.

Tagliatelle alla Bolognese

Tagliatelle with Meat Sauce

THIS RECIPE IS AN authentic meat sauce – ragù – from the city of Bologna in Emilia-Romagna. It is very rich, and is always served with tagliatelle, never with spaghetti.

INGREDIENTS

450g/1lb fresh or dried tagliatelle
salt and ground black pepper
freshly grated Parmesan cheese, to serve

For the Bolognese meat sauce

1 onion
2 carrots
2 celery sticks
2 garlic cloves
25g/1oz/2 tbsp butter
15ml/1 tbsp olive oil
130g/4¹/₂oz pancetta or rindless streaky bacon, diced
250g/9oz lean minced beef
250g/9oz lean minced pork
120ml/4fl oz/¹/₂ cup dry white wine
2 x 400g/14oz cans crushed Italian plum tomatoes
475–750ml/16fl oz–1¹/₄ pints/2–3 cups beef stock
100ml/3¹/₂fl oz/scant ¹/₂ cup panna da cucina or double cream
Serves 6–8

2 Add the minced beef and pork, lower the heat and cook gently for 10 minutes, stirring frequently and breaking up any lumps in the meat with a wooden spoon. Stir in salt and pepper to taste, then add the wine and stir again. Simmer for about 5 minutes, or until reduced.

4 Pour the cream into the sauce, stir well to mix, then simmer, without a lid, for another 30 minutes, stirring frequently. Meanwhile, cook the pasta according to the packet instructions. Taste the sauce to check the seasoning. Drain the cooked pasta and tip it into a warmed bowl. Pour the sauce over the pasta and toss well. Serve immediately, sprinkled with grated Parmesan.

1 Make the meat sauce. Chop all the fresh vegetables finely,. Heat the butter and oil in a large skillet or saucepan until sizzling. Add the vegetables and the pancetta or bacon and cook over a medium heat, stirring frequently, for 10 minutes or until the vegetables have softened.

3 Add the canned tomatoes and 250ml/8fl oz/1 cup of the beef stock and bring to the boil. Stir the sauce well, then lower the heat. Half cover the pan with a lid and leave to simmer very gently for 2 hours. Stir occasionally during this time and add more stock as it becomes absorbed.

VARIATION

Some cooks add a few chopped chicken livers when frying the meat at the beginning of Step 2. This gives the sauce a stronger, almost gamey, flavour.

Spaghetti con Polpettine

Spaghetti with Meatballs

MEATBALLS SIMMERED IN A sweet and spicy tomato sauce are truly delicious with spaghetti. Children love them and you can easily leave out the chillies.

INGREDIENTS

350g/12oz minced beef
1 egg
*60ml/4 tbsp roughly chopped fresh flat
    leaf parsley*
2.5ml/1/2 tsp crushed dried red chillies
1 thick slice white bread, crusts removed
30ml/2 tbsp milk
about 30ml/2 tbsp olive oil
300ml/1/2 pint/1 1/4 cups passata
400ml/14fl oz/1 3/4 cups vegetable stock
5ml/1 tsp granulated sugar
*350–450g/12oz–1lb fresh or
    dried spaghetti*
salt and ground black pepper
freshly grated Parmesan cheese, to serve
Serves 6–8

1 Put the minced beef in a large bowl. Add the egg, and half the parsley and half the crushed chillies. Season with plenty of salt and pepper.

2 Tear the bread into small pieces and place in a small bowl. Moisten with the milk. Leave to soak for a few minutes, then squeeze out the excess milk and crumble the bread over the meat mixture. Mix everything together with a wooden spoon, then use your hands to squeeze and knead the mixture so that it becomes smooth and quite sticky.

3 Wash your hands, rinse them under the cold tap, then pick up small pieces of the mixture and roll them between your palms to make about 40–60 small balls. Place the meatballs on a tray and chill in the fridge for about 30 minutes.

4 Heat the oil in a large non-stick frying pan. Cook the meatballs in batches until browned on all sides. Pour the passata and stock into a large saucepan. Heat gently, then add the remaining chillies and the sugar, with salt and pepper to taste. Add the meatballs to the passata mixture, then bring to the boil. Lower the heat and cover. Simmer for 20 minutes.

5 Cook the pasta according to the packet instructions. When it is *al dente*, drain and tip it into a warmed large bowl. Pour the sauce over the pasta and toss gently. Sprinkle with the remaining parsley and serve with grated Parmesan handed separately.

Lamb and Sweet Pepper Sauce

THIS SIMPLE SAUCE is a speciality of the Abruzzo-Molise region, east of Rome, where it is traditionally served with *maccheroni alla chitarra* – square-shaped long macaroni.

INGREDIENTS

60ml/4 tbsp olive oil

250g/9oz boneless lamb neck fillet, diced quite small

2 garlic cloves, finely chopped

2 bay leaves, torn

250ml/8fl oz/1 cup dry white wine

4 ripe Italian plum tomatoes, peeled and chopped

2 large red peppers, seeded and diced

salt and ground black pepper

Serves 4–6

1 Heat half the olive oil in a medium skillet or saucepan, add the small pieces of lamb and sprinkle with a little salt and pepper. Cook the meat over a medium to high heat for about 10 minutes, stirring often, until it is browned on all sides.

2 Sprinkle in the garlic and add the bay leaves, then pour in the wine and let it bubble until reduced.

3 Add the remaining oil, the tomatoes and the peppers; stir to mix with the lamb. Season again. Cover with the lid and simmer over a low heat for 45–55 minutes or until the lamb is very tender. Stir occasionally during cooking and moisten with water if the sauce becomes too dry. Remove the bay leaves from the sauce before serving it with pasta.

COOK'S TIPS

• *The peppers don't have to be red. Use yellow, orange or green if you prefer; either one colour or a mixture.*

• *If you need to add water to the sauce towards the end of cooking, take it from the pan used for cooking the pasta.*

• *You can make your own fresh* maccheroni alla chitarra *or buy the dried pasta from an Italian delicatessen. Alternatively, this sauce is just as good with ordinary long or short macaroni. You will need 350–425g/12–15oz.*

Fusilli con Salsicce
Fusilli with Sausage

SPICY HOT SAUSAGE and tomato sauce combine with spirals of pasta to make this really tasty dish from southern Italy. Pecorino cheese, with its strong and salty flavour, is the perfect accompaniment. Serve for an informal supper party with a full-bodied red wine and crusty country bread.

INGREDIENTS

400g/14oz spicy pork sausages
30ml/2 tbsp olive oil
1 small onion, finely chopped
2 garlic cloves, crushed
1 large yellow pepper, seeded and cut
   into strips
5ml/1 tsp paprika
5ml/1 tsp dried mixed herbs
5–10ml/1–2 tsp chilli sauce
400g/14oz can Italian plum tomatoes
250–300ml/8–10fl oz/1–1¼ cups
   vegetable stock
300g/11oz/2¾ cups fresh or dried fusilli
salt and ground black pepper
freshly grated Pecorino cheese, to serve
Serves 4

1 Grill the sausages for 10–12 minutes until they are browned on all sides, then drain them on kitchen paper.

2 Heat the oil in a large skillet or saucepan, add the onion and garlic and cook over a low heat, stirring frequently, for 5–7 minutes until soft. Add the yellow pepper, paprika, herbs and chilli sauce to taste. Cook gently for 5–7 minutes, stirring occasionally.

3 Tip in the canned tomatoes, breaking them up with a wooden spoon, then add salt and pepper to taste and stir well. Cook over a medium heat for 10–12 minutes, adding the vegetable stock gradually as the sauce reduces.

4 While the tomato sauce is cooking, cut the grilled sausages diagonally into 1cm/½in pieces.

5 Add the sausage pieces to the sauce, reduce the heat to low and cook for 10 minutes. Meanwhile, cook the pasta according to the instructions on the packet.

6 Taste the sauce for seasoning. Drain the pasta and add it to the pan of sauce. Toss well, then divide among four warmed bowls. Sprinkle each serving with a little grated Pecorino and serve immediately, with more Pecorino handed separately.

Malloreddus

Sardinian Sausage and Pasta

IN SARDINIA THEY CALL this dish simply "malloreddus", which is the local name for the type of pasta traditionally used to make it.

INGREDIENTS

30ml/2 tbsp olive oil

6 garlic cloves

200g/7oz Italian pure pork sausage, diced small

2 small handfuls fresh basil leaves

400g/14oz can chopped Italian plum tomatoes

a good pinch of saffron threads

15ml/1 tbsp granulated sugar

350g/12oz/3 cups dried malloreddus (gnocchi sardi)

75g/3oz/1 cup freshly grated Pecorino Sardo cheese

salt and ground black pepper

Serves 4–6

1 Heat the oil in a medium skillet or saucepan. Add the garlic, sausage and half the basil leaves. Fry, stirring frequently, until the sausage is browned all over. Remove and discard the garlic. Add the tomatoes. Fill the empty can with water, pour it into the pan, then stir in the saffron, sugar, 5ml/1 tsp salt and pepper to taste. Bring to the boil, lower the heat and simmer for 20–30 minutes, stirring occasionally.

2 Meanwhile, cook the pasta in a pan of salted boiling water according to the packet instructions.

3 Drain the pasta and tip it into a warmed bowl. Taste the sauce for seasoning, pour it over the pasta and toss well. Add about one-third of the grated Pecorino and the remaining basil and toss well to mix again. Serve immediately, with the remaining pecorino sprinkled on top.

COOK'S TIP

In Sardinia, a special type of sausage is used for malloreddus. It is flavoured with aniseed and black pepper and is called sartizzu sardo. A good alternative to sartizzu sardo would be the piquant salsiccia piccante. If, however, you prefer a slightly milder flavour, try luganega, which is much more widely available. Some butchers make their own Italian-style sausage on the premises, in which case you can always ask the butcher if he will season it for you with aniseed and black pepper if you want to try and create the authentic taste for yourself.

Rigatoni alla Bresàola e Peperoni

Rigatoni with Bresàola and Peppers

BRESÀOLA – CURED RAW BEEF – is usually served thinly sliced as an antipasto. Here its strong, almost gamey, flavour is used to good effect.

INGREDIENTS

30ml/2 tbsp olive oil

1 small onion, finely chopped

150g/5oz bresàola, cut into thin strips

4 peppers (red and orange or yellow), diced

120ml/4fl oz/1/2 cup dry white wine

400g/14oz can chopped plum tomatoes

450g/1lb/4 cups dried rigatoni

50g/2oz/2/3 cup freshly shaved Parmesan cheese

1 small handful fresh basil leaves

salt and ground black pepper

Serves 6

1 Heat the oil in a medium saucepan, add the onion and *bresàola*. Cover the pan and cook over a low heat for 5–8 minutes until the onion has softened. Add the peppers, wine, 5ml/1 tsp salt and plenty of pepper. Stir well, then simmer for 10–15 minutes.

2 Add the canned tomatoes to the pan and increase the heat to high. Bring to the boil, stirring, then lower the heat and replace the lid again. Simmer gently, stirring occasionally, for 20 minutes or until the peppers are very soft and quite creamy. Meanwhile, cook the pasta in a pan of salted boiling water according to the instructions on the packet.

3 Drain the cooked pasta and tip it into a warmed bowl. Taste the sauce for seasoning, then pour it over the pasta and add half the Parmesan. Toss well and serve immediately, with the basil leaves and the remaining Parmesan sprinkled on top.

Fettuccine al Prosciutto e Piselli

Fettuccine with Ham and Peas

THIS SIMPLE DISH MAKES a very good first course for six people, or a main course for three to four. The ingredients are all easily available from the supermarket, so the recipe makes an ideal impromptu supper.

INGREDIENTS
50g/2oz/¼ cup butter
1 small onion, finely chopped
200g/7oz/1¾ cups fresh or frozen peas
100ml/3½fl oz/scant ½ cup
  chicken stock
2.5ml/½ tsp granulated sugar
175ml/6fl oz/¾ cup dry white wine
350g/12oz fresh fettuccine
75g/3oz piece cooked ham, cut into
  bite-size chunks
115g/4oz/1⅓ cups freshly grated
  Parmesan cheese
salt and ground black pepper
Serves 3–6

1 Melt the butter in a medium skillet or saucepan, add the onion and cook over a low heat for about 5 minutes until softened but not coloured. Add the peas, stock and sugar, with salt and pepper to taste.

2 Bring to the boil, then lower the heat and simmer for 3–5 minutes or until the peas are tender. Add the wine, increase the heat and boil until the wine has reduced.

3 Cook the pasta according to the instructions on the packet. When it is almost ready, add the ham to the sauce, with about a third of the grated Parmesan. Heat through, stirring, then taste for seasoning.

4 Drain the pasta and tip it into a warmed large bowl. Pour the sauce over the pasta and toss well. Serve immediately, sprinkled with the remaining grated Parmesan.

Rigatoni con Ragù di Maiale
Rigatoni with Pork

THIS IS AN EXCELLENT meat sauce using minced pork rather than the more usual minced beef. Here it is served with rigatoni, a short tubular pasta shape, but you could serve it with tagliatelle or spaghetti to make a pork version of Bolognese.

INGREDIENTS

1 small onion
1/2 carrot
1/2 celery stick
2 garlic cloves
25g/1oz/2 tbsp butter
30ml/2 tbsp olive oil
150g/5oz minced pork
60ml/4 tbsp dry white wine
400g/14oz can chopped Italian
  plum tomatoes
a few fresh basil leaves, plus extra basil
  leaves, to garnish
400g/14oz/3 1/2 cups dried rigatoni
salt and ground black pepper
freshly shaved Parmesan cheese,
  to serve

Serves 4

1 Chop all the fresh vegetables finely, either in a food processor or by hand. Heat the butter and oil in a large skillet or saucepan until just sizzling, add the chopped vegetables and cook over a medium heat, stirring frequently, for 3–4 minutes.

2 Add the minced pork and cook gently for 2–3 minutes, breaking up any lumps in the meat with a wooden spoon.

3 Lower the heat and fry for a further 2–3 minutes, stirring frequently, then stir in the wine. Mix in the tomatoes, whole basil leaves, salt to taste and plenty of pepper. Bring to the boil, then lower the heat, cover and simmer for 40 minutes, stirring from time to time.

4 Cook the pasta according to the instructions on the packet. Just before draining it, add a ladleful or two of the cooking water to the sauce. Stir well, then taste the sauce for seasoning.

5 Drain the pasta, add it to the pan of sauce and toss well. Serve immediately, sprinkled with the basil and shaved Parmesan.

VARIATION

To give the sauce a more intense flavour, soak 15g/1/2oz dried porcini mushrooms in 175ml/6fl oz/3/4 cup warm water for 15–20 minutes, then drain, chop and add with the meat.

Eliche con Salsiccie e Radicchio

Eliche with Sausage and Radicchio

SAUSAGE AND RADICCHIO may seem odd companions, but the combined flavour of these ingredients is really delicious. This robust and hearty dish makes a good main course.

INGREDIENTS

30ml/2 tbsp olive oil
1 onion, finely chopped
200g/7oz Italian pure pork sausage
175ml/6fl oz/3/4 cup passata
90ml/6 tbsp dry white wine
300g/11oz/2³/4 cups dried eliche
50g/2oz radicchio leaves
salt and ground black pepper
Serves 4

1 Heat the olive oil in a large, deep skillet or saucepan. Add the finely chopped onion and cook over a low heat, stirring frequently, for about 5 minutes until softened.

2 Snip the end off the sausage skin and squeeze the sausagemeat into the pan. With a wooden spoon, stir the sausagemeat to mix it with the oil and onion and break it up into small pieces.

3 Continue to fry the mixture, increasing the heat if necessary, until the sausagemeat is brown all over and looks crumbly. Stir in the passata, then sprinkle in the wine, with salt and pepper to taste. Simmer over a low heat, stirring occasionally, for 10–12 minutes.

4 Meanwhile, cook the pasta according to the instructions on the packet. Just before draining the pasta, add a ladleful or two of the cooking water to the sausage sauce and stir it in well. Taste the sauce to check the seasoning.

5 Finely shred the radicchio leaves. Drain the cooked pasta and tip it into the pan of sausage sauce. Add the shredded radicchio and toss well to combine everything together. Serve immediately.

COOK'S TIPS

• *The best sausage to use is the one you buy from the Italian delicatessen called* salsiccia puro suino. *It is made from 100 per cent pure pork plus flavourings and seasonings.*
• *If you can get it, use the long, tapering* radicchio di Treviso *for this dish; otherwise the tightly furled, round radicchio can be used.*

Spaghetti Bolognese

Spaghetti with Minced Beef Sauce

SPAGHETTI BOLOGNESE is not an authentic Italian dish. It was "invented" by Italian emigrés in America in the sixties in response to popular demand for a spaghetti dish with meat sauce. This is a rich, spicy version.

INGREDIENTS

30ml/2 tbsp olive oil
1 onion, finely chopped
1 garlic clove, crushed
5ml/1 tsp dried mixed herbs
1.25ml/¼ tsp cayenne pepper
350–450g/12oz–1lb minced beef
400g/14oz can chopped Italian
   plum tomatoes
45ml/3 tbsp tomato ketchup
15ml/1 tbsp sun-dried tomato paste
5ml/1 tsp Worcestershire sauce
5ml/1 tsp dried oregano
450ml/¾ pint/1¾ cups beef or
   vegetable stock
45ml/3 tbsp red wine
400–450g/14oz–1lb dried spaghetti
salt and ground black pepper
freshly grated Parmesan cheese, to serve

Serves 4–6

2 Stir in the canned tomatoes, ketchup, sun-dried tomato paste, Worcestershire sauce, oregano and plenty of black pepper. Pour in the stock and red wine and bring to the boil, stirring. Cover the pan, lower the heat and leave the sauce to simmer for 30 minutes, stirring occasionally.

3 Cook the pasta according to the instructions on the packet. Drain well and divide among warmed bowls. Taste the sauce and add a little salt if necessary, then spoon it on top of the pasta and sprinkle with a little grated Parmesan. Serve immediately, with grated Parmesan handed separately.

1 Heat the oil in a medium saucepan, add the onion and garlic and cook over a low heat, stirring frequently, for about 5 minutes until softened. Stir in the mixed herbs and cayenne and cook for 2–3 minutes more. Add the minced beef and cook gently for about 5 minutes, stirring frequently and breaking up any lumps in the meat with a wooden spoon.

Farfalle con Pollo e Pomodorini

Farfalle with Chicken and Cherry Tomatoes

QUICK TO PREPARE and easy to cook, this colourful dish is full of flavour. Serve it for a midweek supper, with a green salad to follow.

INGREDIENTS

350g/12oz skinless chicken breast fillets,
*   cut into bite-size pieces*
60ml/4 tbsp Italian dry vermouth
10ml/2 tsp chopped fresh rosemary, plus
*   4 fresh rosemary sprigs, to garnish*
15ml/1 tbsp olive oil
1 onion, finely chopped
90g/3¹/₂oz piece Italian salami, diced
275g/10oz/2¹/₂ cups dried farfalle
15ml/1 tbsp balsamic vinegar
400g/14oz can Italian cherry tomatoes
good pinch of crushed dried red chillies
salt and ground black pepper

Serves 4

1 Put the pieces of chicken in a large bowl, pour in the dry vermouth and sprinkle with half the chopped rosemary and salt and pepper to taste. Stir well and set aside.

2 Heat the oil in a large skillet or saucepan, add the onion and salami and fry over a medium heat for about 5 minutes, stirring frequently.

3 Cook the pasta according to the instructions on the packet.

4 Add the chicken and vermouth to the onion and salami, increase the heat to high and fry for 3 minutes or until the chicken is white on all sides. Sprinkle the vinegar over the chicken.

5 Add the cherry tomatoes and dried chillies. Stir well and simmer for a few minutes more. Taste the sauce for seasoning.

6 Drain the pasta and tip it into the skillet or saucepan. Add the remaining chopped rosemary and toss to mix the pasta and sauce together. Serve immediately in warmed bowls, garnished with the rosemary sprigs.

COOK'S TIP

The tomatoes look good left whole, but if you prefer you can crush them with the back of a wooden spoon while they are simmering in the pan.

Pappardelle con Sugo di Coniglio

Pappardelle with Rabbit Sauce

THIS RICH-TASTING DISH comes from the north of Italy, where rabbit sauces for pasta are very popular.

INGREDIENTS

15g/½oz dried porcini mushrooms

175ml/6fl oz/¾ cup warm water

1 small onion

½ carrot

½ celery stick

2 bay leaves

25g/1oz/2 tbsp butter

15ml/1 tbsp olive oil

40g/1½oz pancetta or rindless streaky
   bacon, chopped

15ml/1 tbsp roughly chopped fresh flat
   leaf parsley, plus extra to garnish

250g/9oz boneless rabbit meat

90ml/6 tbsp dry white wine

200g/7oz can chopped Italian plum
   tomatoes or 200ml/7fl oz/scant
   1 cup passata

300g/11oz fresh or dried pappardelle

salt and ground black pepper

Serves 4

1 Put the dried mushrooms in a bowl, pour over the warm water and leave to soak for 15–20 minutes. Finely chop the vegetables, either in a food processor or by hand. Make a tear in each bay leaf, so that they will release their flavour when added to the sauce.

2 Heat the butter and oil in a skillet or medium saucepan until just sizzling. Add the chopped vegetables, pancetta or bacon and the parsley and cook for about 5 minutes.

3 Add the pieces of rabbit and fry on both sides for 3–4 minutes. Pour the wine over and let it reduce for a few minutes, then add the tomatoes or passata. Drain the mushrooms and pour the soaking liquid into the pan. Chop the mushrooms and add them to the mixture, with the bay leaves and salt and pepper to taste. Stir well, cover and simmer for 35–40 minutes until the rabbit is tender, stirring occasionally.

4 Remove the pan from the heat and lift out the pieces of rabbit with a slotted spoon. Cut them into bite-size chunks and stir them into the sauce. Remove and discard the bay leaves. Taste the sauce and add more salt and pepper, if needed. Cook the pasta according to the instructions on the packet. Meanwhile, reheat the sauce. Drain the pasta and toss with the sauce in a warmed bowl. Serve immediately, sprinkled with parsley.

Pappardelle al Pollo e Porcini

Pappardelle with Chicken and Mushrooms

RICH AND CREAMY, this is a good supper party dish.

INGREDIENTS

15g/¹/₂oz dried porcini mushrooms
175ml/6fl oz/³/₄ cup warm water
25g/1oz/2 tbsp butter
1 garlic clove, crushed
1 small handful fresh flat leaf parsley,
  roughly chopped
1 small leek or 4 spring onions, chopped
120ml/4fl oz/¹/₂ cup dry white wine
250ml/8fl oz/1 cup chicken stock
400g/14oz fresh or dried pappardelle
2 skinless chicken breast fillets, cut into
  thin strips
105ml/7 tbsp mascarpone cheese
salt and ground black pepper
fresh basil leaves, shredded, to garnish

Serves 4

1 Put the dried mushrooms in a bowl. Pour in the warm water and leave to soak for 15–20 minutes. Tip into a fine sieve set over a bowl and squeeze the mushrooms with your hands to release as much liquid as possible.

2 Chop the mushrooms finely and set aside the strained soaking liquid until required.

3 Melt the butter in a medium skillet or saucepan, add the chopped mushrooms, garlic, parsley and leek or spring onions, with salt and pepper to taste. Cook over a low heat, stirring frequently, for about 5 minutes, then pour in the wine and stock and bring to the boil. Lower the heat and simmer for about 5 minutes or until the liquid has reduced and is thickened.

4 Meanwhile, start cooking the pasta in salted boiling water according to the packet instructions, adding the reserved soaking liquid from the mushrooms to the water.

5 Add the chicken strips to the sauce and simmer for 5 minutes or until just tender. Add the mascarpone a spoonful at a time, stirring well after each addition, then add one or two spoonfuls of the water used for cooking the pasta. Taste for seasoning.

6 Drain the pasta and tip it into a warmed large bowl. Add the chicken and sauce and toss well. Serve immediately, topped with the shredded basil leaves.

VARIATIONS

• *Add 115g/4oz/1 cup sliced button or chestnut mushrooms with the chicken.*
• *Add blanched sprigs of broccoli before the mascarpone in Step 5.*

Conchiglie coi Fegatini alle Erbe

Conchiglie with Chicken Livers and Herbs

FRESH HERBS AND CHICKEN livers are a good combination, often used together on crostini in Tuscany. Here they are tossed with pasta shells to make a very tasty supper dish.

INGREDIENTS

50g/2oz/¹/4 cup butter

115g/4oz pancetta or rindless streaky bacon, diced

250g/9oz frozen chicken livers, thawed, drained and diced

2 garlic cloves, crushed

10ml/2 tsp chopped fresh sage

300g/11oz/2³/4 cups dried conchiglie

150ml/¹/4 pint/²/3 cup dry white wine

4 ripe Italian plum tomatoes, peeled and diced

15ml/1 tbsp chopped fresh flat leaf parsley

salt and ground black pepper

Serves 4

1 Melt half the butter in a medium skillet or saucepan, add the pancetta or bacon and fry over a medium heat for a few minutes until it is lightly coloured but not crisp.

2 Add the chicken livers, garlic, half the sage and plenty of pepper. Increase the heat and toss the livers for about 5 minutes, until they change colour all over. Meanwhile, start cooking the pasta according to the instructions on the packet.

3 Pour the wine over the chicken livers in the pan and let it sizzle, then lower the heat and simmer gently for 5 minutes. Add the remaining butter to the pan. As soon as it has melted, add the diced tomatoes, toss to mix, then add the remaining sage and the parsley. Stir well. Taste and add salt if needed.

4 Drain the pasta and tip it into a warmed bowl. Pour the sauce over and toss well. Serve immediately.

Pasta Salads

Although not traditionally Italian, pasta salads have earned their place in the Italian cook's repertoire. They are extremely versatile in that they can be served as part of an antipasto, as a first course or a main course. Salads can be prepared well in advance, so make marvellous party food, and are popular for picnics, because they are so easy to transport.

Freshly cooked pasta soaks up oil, lemon juice, vinegar and seasonings so that when the pasta cools down, the shapes are separate, moist and full of flavour. Never soak pasta in cold water after cooking; this makes the pasta waterlogged and soggy, especially with shapes like shells and tubes that trap liquid. Simply cook the pasta until it is *al dente*, then drain it thoroughly and toss it in extra virgin olive oil or dressing until it glistens. This method works well for any vinaigrette-type dressing, but if you are using mayonnaise it is best to wait until the pasta has cooled down before tossing, or the mayonnaise may spoil.

Any pasta shape can be used in a salad, although shells and tubes are particularly good, because they trap the dressing so well. Many Italians prefer egg pasta to plain durum wheat pasta, because it has a good colour, holds its shape well and does not stick.

Insalata Nizzarda

Pasta Salade Niçoise

ALONG THE MEDITERRANEAN coast, where Italy meets France, the cuisines of both countries have many similarities. In this salad the ingredients of a classic French *salade niçoise* are given a modern Italian twist.

INGREDIENTS

115g/4oz French beans, topped and tailed
    and cut into 5cm/2in lengths
250g/9oz/2¼ cups dried penne rigate
105ml/7 tbsp extra virgin olive oil
2 fresh tuna steaks, total weight
    350–450g/12oz–1lb
6 baby Italian plum tomatoes, quartered
    lengthways
50g/2oz/½ cup pitted black olives,
    halved lengthways
6 bottled or canned anchovies in olive oil,
    drained and chopped
30–45ml/2–3 tbsp chopped fresh flat leaf
    parsley, to taste
juice of ½–1 lemon, to taste
2 heads of chicory, leaves
    separated
salt and ground black pepper
lemon wedges, to serve

Serves 4

1 Cook the beans in a large pan of salted boiling water for 5–6 minutes. Remove the beans with a large slotted spoon and refresh under the cold tap.

2 Add the pasta to the pan of bean cooking water, bring back to the boil and cook according to the instructions on the packet.

3 Meanwhile, heat a ridged cast-iron pan over a low heat. Dip a wad of kitchen paper in the oil, wipe it over the surface of the pan and heat gently. Brush the tuna steaks on both sides with oil and sprinkle liberally with pepper; add to the pan and cook over a medium to high heat for 1–2 minutes on each side. Remove and set aside.

4 Drain the cooked pasta well and tip into a large bowl. Add the remaining oil, the beans, tomato quarters, black olives, anchovies, parsley, lemon juice and salt and pepper to taste. Toss well to mix, then leave to cool.

5 Flake or slice the tuna into large pieces, discarding the skin, then fold it into the salad. Taste the salad for seasoning. Arrange the chicory leaves around the insides of a large shallow bowl. Spoon the pasta salad into the centre and serve with lemon wedges.

Chargrilled Pepper Salad

THIS IS A GOOD SIDE SALAD to serve with plain grilled or barbecued chicken or fish. The ingredients are simple and few, but the overall flavour is quite intense.

INGREDIENTS

2 large peppers (red and green)
250g/9oz/2 1/4 cups dried fusilli tricolore
1 handful fresh basil leaves
1 handful fresh coriander leaves
1 garlic clove
salt and ground black pepper

For the dressing
30ml/2 tbsp bottled pesto
juice of 1/2 lemon
60ml/4 tbsp extra virgin olive oil
Serves 4

1 Put the peppers under a hot grill and grill them for about 10 minutes, turning them frequently until they are charred on all sides. Put the hot peppers in a plastic bag, seal the bag and set aside until the peppers are cool. Meanwhile, cook the pasta according to the instructions on the packet.

2 Whisk all the dressing ingredients together in a large bowl. Drain the cooked pasta well and tip it into the bowl of dressing. Toss well to mix and set aside to cool.

COOK'S TIP

Serve the salad at room temperature or chilled, whichever you prefer.

3 Remove the peppers from the bag and hold them one at a time under cold running water. Peel off the charred skins with your fingers, split the peppers open and pull out the cores. Rub off all the seeds under the running water, then pat the peppers dry on kitchen paper.

4 Chop the peppers and add them to the pasta. Put the basil, coriander and garlic on a board and chop them all together. Add to the pasta and toss to mix, then taste for seasoning and serve.

Insalata con Tonno e Mais
Tuna and Sweetcorn Salad

THIS IS AN EXCELLENT main course salad for a summer lunch outside. It travels very well, so it is good for picnics, too.

INGREDIENTS
175g/6oz/1 1/2 cups dried conchiglie
175g/6oz can tuna in olive oil, drained and flaked
175g/6oz can sweetcorn, drained
75g/3oz bottled roasted red pepper, rinsed, dried and finely chopped
1 handful of fresh basil leaves, chopped
salt and ground black pepper

For the dressing
60ml/4 tbsp extra virgin olive oil
15ml/1 tbsp balsamic vinegar
5ml/1 tsp red wine vinegar
5ml/1 tsp Dijon mustard
5–10ml/1–2 tsp honey, to taste
Serves 4

1 Cook the pasta according to packet instructions. Drain it into a colander, and rinse under cold running water. Leave to drain until cold and dry, shaking the colander occasionally.

2 Make the dressing. Put the oil in a large bowl, add the two kinds of vinegar and whisk well together until emulsified. Add the mustard, honey and salt and pepper to taste and whisk again until thick.

3 Add the pasta to the dressing and toss well to mix, then add the tuna, sweetcorn and roasted pepper and toss again. Mix in about half the basil and taste for seasoning. Serve at room temperature or chilled, with the remaining basil sprinkled on top.

VARIATION

To save time, you could use canned sweetcorn with peppers.

Insalata Rosa e Verde
Pink and Green Salad

SPIKED WITH A LITTLE fresh chilli, this pretty salad makes a delicious light lunch served with hot ciabatta rolls and a bottle of sparkling dry Italian white wine. Prawns and avocado are a winning combination, so it's also a good choice for a buffet party.

INGREDIENTS
225g/8oz/2 cups dried farfalle
juice of 1/2 lemon
1 small fresh red chilli, seeded and very finely chopped
60ml/4 tbsp chopped fresh basil
30ml/2 tbsp chopped fresh coriander
60ml/4 tbsp extra virgin olive oil
15ml/1 tbsp mayonnaise
250g/9oz/1 1/2 cups peeled cooked prawns
1 avocado
salt and ground black pepper
Serves 4

1 Cook the pasta in a large saucepan of salted boiling water according to the packet instructions.

2 Meanwhile, put the lemon juice and chilli in a bowl with half the basil and coriander and salt and pepper to taste. Whisk well to mix, then whisk in the oil and mayonnaise until thick. Add the prawns and gently stir to coat in the dressing.

3 Drain the pasta into a colander, and rinse under cold running water until cold. Leave to drain and dry, shaking the colander occasionally.

4 Halve, stone and peel the avocado, then cut the flesh into neat dice. Add to the prawns and dressing with the pasta, toss well to mix and taste for seasoning. Serve immediately, sprinkled with the remaining basil and coriander.

COOK'S TIP

This pasta salad can be made several hours ahead of time, without the avocado. Cover the bowl with clear film and chill in the fridge. Prepare the avocado and add it to the salad just before serving or it will discolour.

Insalata di Mare

Seafood Salad

THIS IS A VERY SPECIAL SALAD which can be served as a first course or main meal. The choice of pasta shape is up to you, but one of the unusual "designer" shapes would suit it well.

INGREDIENTS

450g/1lb mussels
250ml/8fl oz/1 cup dry white wine
2 garlic cloves, roughly chopped
1 handful of fresh flat leaf parsley
175g/6oz/1 cup prepared squid rings
175g/6oz/1½ cups small dried
  pasta shapes
175g/6oz/1 cup peeled cooked prawns

For the dressing
90ml/6 tbsp extra virgin olive oil
juice of 1 lemon
5–10ml/1–2 tsp capers, to taste,
  roughly chopped
1 garlic clove, crushed
1 small handful fresh flat leaf parsley,
  finely chopped
salt and ground black pepper
Serves 4–6

1 Scrub the mussels under cold running water to remove the beards. Discard any that are open or that do not close when sharply tapped against the work surface.

2 Pour half the wine into a large saucepan, add the garlic, parsley and mussels. Cover the pan tightly and bring to the boil over a high heat. Cook for about 5 minutes, shaking the pan frequently, until the mussels are open.

3 Tip the mussels and their liquid into a colander set over a bowl . Leave the mussels until cool enough to handle. Reserve a few mussels for garnishing, then remove the rest from their shells, tipping the liquid from the mussels into the bowl of cooking liquid. Discard any closed mussels.

4 Return the mussel cooking liquid to the pan and add the remaining wine and the squid rings. Bring to the boil, cover and simmer gently, stirring occasionally, for 30 minutes or until the squid is tender. Leave the squid to cool in the cooking liquid.

5 Meanwhile, cook the pasta according to packet instructions and whisk all the dressing ingredients in a large bowl, adding a little salt and pepper to taste.

6 Drain the cooked pasta well, add it to the bowl of dressing and toss well to mix. Leave to cool.

7 Tip the cooled squid into a sieve and drain well, then rinse it lightly under the cold tap. Add the squid, mussels and prawns to the dressed pasta and toss well to mix. Cover the bowl tightly with clear film and chill in the fridge for about 4 hours. Toss well and adjust the seasoning to taste before serving.

COOK'S TIP

For a quick and easy short cut, buy ready-prepared seafood salad from an Italian delicatessen and toss it with the pasta and dressing.

Insalata con Pomodori Arrostiti e Rucola

Roasted Cherry Tomato and Rocket Salad

THIS IS A GOOD SIDE SALAD to accompany barbecued chicken, steaks or chops. Roasted tomatoes are very juicy, with an intense, smoky-sweet flavour.

INGREDIENTS

225g/8oz/2 cups dried chifferini or pipe

450g/1lb ripe baby Italian plum tomatoes, halved lengthways

75ml/5 tbsp extra virgin olive oil

2 garlic cloves, cut into thin slivers

30ml/2 tbsp balsamic vinegar

2 pieces sun-dried tomato in olive oil, drained and chopped

large pinch of sugar, to taste

1 handful rocket, about 65g/2½oz

salt and ground black pepper

Serves 4

1 Preheat the oven to 190°C/375°F/ Gas 5. Meanwhile, cook the pasta in salted boiling water according to the instructions on the packet.

2 Arrange the halved tomatoes cut side up in a roasting tin, drizzle 30ml/2tbsp of the oil over them and sprinkle with the slivers of garlic and salt and pepper to taste. Roast in the oven for 20 minutes, turning once.

3 Put the remaining oil in a large bowl with the vinegar, sun-dried tomatoes, sugar and a little salt and pepper to taste. Stir well to mix. Drain the pasta, add it to the bowl of dressing and toss to mix. Add the roasted tomatoes and mix gently.

4 Before serving, add the chopped rocket, toss lightly and taste for seasoning. Serve either at room temperature or chilled.

VARIATIONS

• *If you are in a hurry and don't have time to roast the tomatoes, you can make the salad with halved raw tomatoes instead.*

• *If you like, add 150g/5oz mozzarella cheese, drained and diced, with the rocket in Step 4.*

Insalata Estiva
Summer Salad

RIPE RED TOMATOES, mozzarella and olives make a good base for a fresh and tangy salad that is perfect for a light summer lunch.

INGREDIENTS

350g/12oz/3 cups dried penne

3 ripe tomatoes, diced

150g/5oz packet mozzarella di bufala, drained and diced

10 pitted black olives, sliced

10 pitted green olives, sliced

1 spring onion, thinly sliced on the diagonal

1 handful fresh basil leaves

For the dressing

90ml/6 tbsp extra virgin olive oil

15ml/1 tbsp balsamic vinegar or lemon juice

salt and ground black pepper

Serves 4

1 Cook the pasta according to the instructions on the packet. Tip it into a colander and rinse under cold running water, then shake the colander to remove as much water as possible. Leave the pasta to drain.

2 Make the dressing. Whisk the olive oil and balsamic vinegar or lemon juice in a large bowl with a little salt and pepper to taste.

3 Add the pasta, mozzarella, tomatoes, olives and spring onion to the dressing and toss together well. Taste for seasoning before serving, sprinkled with basil leaves.

COOK'S TIP

Mozzarella made from buffalo milk has more flavour than the type made with cow's milk. It is sold in most delicatessens and supermarkets.

VARIATION

Make the salad more substantial by adding other ingredients, such as sliced peppers, flaked tuna, bottled or canned anchovy fillets or diced ham.

Fusilli Campagnoli
Country Pasta Salad

COLOURFUL, TASTY and nutritious, this is the ideal pasta salad for a summer picnic.

INGREDIENTS

300g/11oz/2¾ cups dried fusilli

150g/5oz French beans, topped and tailed and cut into 5cm/2in lengths

1 potato, about 150g/5oz, diced

200g/7oz baby tomatoes, hulled and halved

2 spring onions, finely chopped

90g/3½oz Parmesan cheese, diced or coarsely shaved

6–8 pitted black olives, cut into rings

15–30ml/1–2 tbsp capers, to taste

For the dressing

90ml/6 tbsp extra virgin olive oil

15ml/1 tbsp balsamic vinegar

15ml/1 tbsp chopped fresh flat leaf parsley

salt and ground black pepper

Serves 6

1 Cook the pasta according to the instructions on the packet. Drain it into a colander, rinse under cold running water until cold, then shake the colander to remove as much water as possible. Leave to drain and dry, shaking the colander occasionally.

2 Cook the beans and diced potato in a saucepan of salted boiling water for 5–6 minutes or until tender. Drain and leave to cool.

3 Make the dressing. Put all the ingredients in a large bowl with salt and pepper to taste and whisk well to mix.

4 Add the baby tomatoes, spring onions, Parmesan, olive rings and capers to the dressing, then the cold pasta, beans and potato. Toss well to mix. Cover and leave to stand for about 30 minutes. Taste for seasoning before serving.

COOK'S TIP

Buy a piece of fresh Parmesan from the delicatessen. This is the less mature, softer type, which is sold as a table cheese, rather than the hard, mature Parmesan used for grating.

Insalata di Pollo e Broccoli

Chicken and Broccoli Salad

GORGONZOLA MAKES A tangy dressing that goes well with both chicken and broccoli. Serve for a lunch or supper dish, with crusty Italian bread.

INGREDIENTS

175g/6oz broccoli florets, divided into
small sprigs
225g/8oz/2 cups dried farfalle
2 large cooked chicken breasts

For the dressing
90g/3¹/₂oz Gorgonzola cheese
15ml/1 tbsp white wine vinegar
60ml/4 tbsp extra virgin olive oil
2.5–5ml/¹/₂–1 tsp finely chopped fresh
sage, plus extra sage sprigs to garnish
salt and ground black pepper

Serves 4

1 Cook the broccoli florets in a large saucepan of salted boiling water for 3 minutes. Remove with a slotted spoon and rinse under cold running water, then spread out on kitchen towels to drain and dry.

2 Add the pasta to the broccoli cooking water, then bring back to the boil and cook according to the packet instructions. When cooked, drain the pasta into a colander, rinse under cold running water until cold, then leave to drain and dry, shaking the colander occasionally.

3 Remove the skin from the cooked chicken breasts and cut the meat into bite-size pieces.

4 Make the dressing. Put the cheese in a large bowl and mash with a fork, then whisk in the wine vinegar followed by the oil and sage and salt and pepper to taste.

5 Add the pasta, chicken and broccoli. Toss well, then season to taste and serve, garnished with sage.

Insalata Saporita

Pasta Salad with Salami and Olives

GARLIC AND HERB DRESSING gives a Mediterranean flavour to a handful of ingredients from the store-cupboard and fridge, making this an excellent salad for winter. There are many different types of Italian salami that can be used. *Salame napoletano* is coarse cut and peppery, while *salame milanese* is fine cut and mild in flavour.

INGREDIENTS

225g/8oz/2 cups dried gnocchi
or conchiglie
50g/2oz/¹/2 cup pitted black olives,
quartered lengthways
75g/3oz thinly sliced salami, any skin
removed, diced
¹/2 small red onion, finely chopped
1 large handful fresh basil leaves

For the dressing
60ml/4 tbsp extra virgin olive oil
good pinch of sugar, to taste
juice of ¹/2 lemon
5ml/1 tsp Dijon mustard
10ml/2 tsp dried oregano
1 garlic clove, crushed
salt and ground black pepper
Serves 4

1 Cook the pasta in a pan of salted boiling water according to the packet instructions.

2 Meanwhile, make the dressing for the pasta. Put all the ingredients for the dressing in a large bowl with a little salt and pepper to taste, and whisk well to mix.

3 Drain the pasta thoroughly, add it to the bowl of dressing and toss well to mix. Leave the dressed pasta to cool, stirring occasionally.

4 When the pasta is cold, add the remaining ingredients and toss well to mix again. Taste for seasoning, then serve immediately.

Penne con la Rucola e la Mozzarella

Penne with Rocket and Mozzarella

LIKE A WARM SALAD, this pasta dish is very quick and easy to make – perfect for an *al fresco* summer lunch. Its success depends on the very best Italian ingredients, so make sure they are as fresh as possible and in tip-top condition.

INGREDIENTS
400g/14oz/3¹/₂ cups fresh or dried penne
6 ripe Italian plum tomatoes, peeled,
*   seeded and diced*
2 x 150g/5oz packets mozzarella cheese,
*   drained and diced*
2 large handfuls of rocket, total weight
*   about 150g/5oz*
75ml/5 tbsp extra virgin olive oil
salt and freshly ground black pepper
Serves 4

1 Cook the pasta in a large saucepan of salted boiling water according to the packet instructions.

2 Meanwhile, put the tomatoes, mozzarella, rocket and olive oil into a large bowl with a little salt and pepper to taste and toss well to mix.

3 Drain the cooked pasta and tip it into the bowl. Toss well to mix and serve immediately.

VARIATION

For a less peppery taste, use basil leaves instead of rocket, or a mixture of the two.

Eliche ai Peperoni Arrostiti

Eliche with Chargrilled Peppers

CHARGRILLED PEPPERS ARE GOOD with pasta because they have a soft juicy texture and a wonderful smoky flavour. This is a dish for high summer when peppers and tomatoes are plentiful and ripe. It is equally good cold as a salad.

INGREDIENTS
3 large peppers (red, yellow
*   and orange)*
350g/12oz/3 cups fresh or dried eliche
*   or fusilli*
1–2 garlic cloves, to taste,
*   finely chopped*
60ml/4 tbsp extra virgin olive oil
4 ripe Italian plum tomatoes, peeled,
*   seeded and diced*
50g/2oz/¹/₂ cup pitted black olives, halved
*   or quartered lengthways*
1 handful of fresh basil leaves
salt and ground black pepper
Serves 4

1 Put the whole peppers under a hot grill and grill them for about 10 minutes, turning them frequently until they are charred on all sides. Put the hot peppers in a plastic bag, seal the bag and set aside until the peppers are cold.

2 Remove the peppers from the bag and hold them one at a time under cold running water. Peel off the charred skins with your fingers, split the peppers open and pull out the cores. Rub off all the seeds under the running water, then pat the peppers dry on kitchen paper.

3 Cook the pasta in a large saucepan of salted boiling water according to the instructions on the packet until *al dente*.

4 Meanwhile, thinly slice the peppers and place them in a large bowl with the remaining ingredients and salt and pepper to taste.

5 Drain the cooked pasta and tip it into the bowl. Toss well to mix and serve immediately.

VARIATION

Add a few slivers of bottled or canned anchovy fillets in Step 4.

Pasta Soups

Soups made with pasta range from clear broths with just a surface scattering of *pastina* to filling and substantial *minestre* or *zuppe*, which include chunkier pieces of pasta and vegetables, fish or meat. Broth, called *brodo* in Italian, is generally served as a first course or *primo piatto*, especially for evening meals. It also makes a marvellous pick-me-up if you are tired, unwell or simply under the weather. The chunkier pasta soups are more likely to make a meal in themselves, especially when served with bread.

This chapter explores the full range of pasta soups. Some, such as *Minestrone alla Genovese* and *Millecosedde*, are regional classics, others are less well known yet equally delicious, but all are gloriously adaptable: use a different shape or size of pasta if you prefer, and don't worry too much about exact quantities.

Cappelletti in Brodo

Little Stuffed Hats in Broth

THIS SOUP IS SERVED in northern Italy on Santo Stefano (St Stephen's Day – our Boxing Day) and on New Year's Day. It makes a welcome light change from all the special celebration food the day before. In Italy, the stock is traditionally made with the Christmas capon carcass.

INGREDIENTS

1.2 litres/2 pints/5 cups chicken stock
90–115g/3½–4oz/1 cup fresh or
   dried cappelletti
30ml/2 tbsp dry white wine (optional)
about 15ml/1 tbsp finely chopped fresh
   flat leaf parsley (optional)
salt and ground black pepper
about 30ml/2 tbsp freshly grated Parmesan
   cheese, to serve
shredded flat leaf parsley, to garnish
Serves 4

1 Pour the chicken stock into a large saucepan and bring to the boil. Add a little salt and pepper to taste, then drop in the pasta.

2 Stir well and bring back to the boil. Lower the heat to a simmer and cook according to the instructions on the packet, until the pasta is *al dente*. Stir frequently during cooking to ensure the pasta cooks evenly.

3 Swirl in the wine and parsley, if using, then taste for seasoning. Ladle into four warmed soup plates, then sprinkle with grated Parmesan and flat leaf parsley. Serve immediately.

COOK'S TIP

Cappelletti is just another name for tortellini, which come from Romagna. You can buy them or make your own.

Pastina in Brodo

Tiny Pasta in Broth

IN ITALY THIS SOUP is often served with bread for a light evening supper.

INGREDIENTS

1.2 litres/2 pints/5 cups beef stock
75g/3oz/¾ cup dried tiny soup pasta,
   e.g. funghetti
2 pieces bottled roasted red pepper, about
   50g/2oz
salt and ground black pepper
coarsely shaved Parmesan cheese, to serve
Serves 4

COOK'S TIP

Stock cubes are not really suitable for a recipe like this in which the flavour of the broth is so important. If you don't have time to make your own stock, use two 300g/11oz cans of condensed beef consommé, adding water as instructed on the labels.

1 Bring the beef stock to the boil in a large saucepan. Add salt and pepper to taste, then drop in the dried soup pasta. Stir well and bring the stock back to the boil.

2 Lower the heat to a simmer and cook until the pasta is *al dente*: 7–8 minutes or according to the packet instructions. Stir frequently during cooking to prevent the pasta shapes from sticking together.

3 Drain the pieces of roasted pepper and dice them finely. Place them in the bottom of four warmed soup plates. Taste the soup for seasoning. Ladle into the soup plates and serve immediately, with shavings of Parmesan handed separately.

VARIATION

You can use other dried tiny soup pastas in place of the funghetti.

Pasta Soups

Genoese Minestrone

In Genoa they often make mine-strone like this, with pesto stirred in towards the end of cooking. It is packed full of vegetables and has a good strong flavour, making it an excellent vegetarian supper dish when served with bread. There is Parmesan cheese in the pesto, so there is no need to serve extra with the soup.

INGREDIENTS

1 onion
2 celery sticks
1 large carrot
45ml/3 tbsp olive oil
150g/5oz French beans, cut into
    5cm/2in pieces
1 courgette, thinly sliced
1 potato, cut into 1cm/¹/₂in cubes
¹/₄ Savoy cabbage, shredded
1 small aubergine, cut into 1cm/¹/₂in cubes
200g/7oz can cannellini beans, drained
    and rinsed
2 Italian plum tomatoes, chopped
1.2 litres/2 pints/5 cups vegetable stock
90g/3¹/₂oz dried vermicelli or spaghetti
salt and ground black pepper

For the pesto

about 20 fresh basil leaves
1 garlic clove
10ml/2 tsp pine nuts
15ml/1 tbsp freshly grated
    Parmesan cheese
15ml/1 tbsp freshly grated
    Pecorino cheese
30ml/2 tbsp olive oil

Serves 4–6

1 Chop the onion, celery and carrot finely, either in a food processor or by hand. Heat the oil in a large saucepan, add the chopped mixture and cook over a low heat, stirring frequently, for 5–7 minutes.

2 Mix in the French beans, courgette, potato and cabbage. Stir-fry over a medium heat for about 3 minutes. Add the aubergine, cannellini beans and tomatoes, and stir-fry for 2–3 minutes more. Pour in the stock with salt and pepper to taste. Bring to the boil. Stir well, cover and lower the heat. Simmer for 40 minutes, stirring occasionally.

3 Meanwhile, process all the pesto ingredients in a food processor until the mixture forms a smooth sauce, adding 15–45ml/1–3 tbsp water through the feeder tube if necessary.

4 Break the pasta into small pieces and add it to the soup. Simmer, stirring frequently, for 5 minutes. Add the pesto sauce and stir it in well, then simmer for 2–3 minutes more, or until the pasta is *al dente*. Taste for seasoning. Serve hot, in warmed soup plates or bowls.

COOK'S TIP

If you don't want to go to the trouble of making your own pesto, use the bottled variety – the traditional green basil pesto rather than the red sun-dried tomato pesto. You will need about 45ml/3 tbsp.

Minestrone Ricco

Rich Minestrone

THIS IS A SPECIAL minestrone made with chicken. Served with crusty Italian bread, it makes a hearty meal.

INGREDIENTS

15ml/1 tbsp olive oil

2 chicken thighs

3 rindless streaky bacon rashers, chopped

1 onion, finely chopped

a few fresh basil leaves, shredded

a few fresh rosemary leaves,
    finely chopped

15ml/1 tbsp chopped fresh flat
    leaf parsley

2 potatoes, cut into 1cm/^{1}/2in cubes

1 large carrot, cut into 1cm/^{1}/2in cubes

2 small courgettes, cut into 1cm/^{1}/2in cubes

1–2 celery sticks, cut into 1cm/^{1}/2in cubes

1 litre/1^3/4 pints/4 cups chicken stock

200g/7oz/1^3/4 cups frozen peas

90g/3^1/2oz/scant 1 cup stellette or other
    dried tiny soup pasta

salt and ground black pepper

coarsely shaved Parmesan cheese, to serve

fresh basil leaves, to garnish

Serves 4–6

1 Heat the oil in a large frying pan, add the chicken thighs and fry for about 5 minutes on each side. Remove with a slotted spoon and set aside.

3 Return the chicken thighs to the pan, add the stock and bring to the boil. Cover and cook over a low heat for 35–40 minutes, stirring the soup occasionally.

5 Meanwhile, remove and discard the chicken skin, then remove the meat from the bones and cut it into 1cm/^{1}/2in pieces. Return the meat to the soup and heat through. Taste for seasoning. Serve hot in soup bowls; scatter over Parmesan shavings and garnish with one or two basil leaves.

2 Lower the heat, add the bacon, onion and herbs to the pan and stir well. Cook gently, stirring constantly, for about 5 minutes. Add all the vegetables, except the frozen peas, and cook for 5–7 minutes more, stirring frequently.

4 Remove the chicken thighs with a slotted spoon and place them on a board. Stir the peas and pasta into the soup and bring back to the boil. Simmer, stirring frequently until the pasta is *al dente*: 7–8 minutes or according to the instructions on the packet.

COOK'S TIP

For extra flavour, add any Parmesan rind to the simmering soup.

Millecosedde

Pasta, Bean and Vegetable Soup

THIS IS A CALABRIAN speciality. The name comes from the Italian word *millecose*, meaning "a thousand things". Literally anything edible can go in this soup. In Calabria they include a bean called *cicerchia* that is peculiar to the region.

INGREDIENTS

75g/3oz/scant $^1/2$ cup brown lentils

15g/$^1/2$oz dried mushrooms

60ml/4 tbsp olive oil

1 carrot, diced

1 celery stick, diced

1 onion, finely chopped

1 garlic clove, finely chopped

a little chopped fresh flat leaf parsley

a good pinch of crushed red chillies (optional)

1.5 litres/2$^1/2$ pints/6$^1/4$ cups vegetable stock

150g/5oz/scant 1 cup each canned red kidney beans, cannellini beans and chick-peas, rinsed and drained

115g/4oz/1 cup dried small pasta shapes, e.g. rigatoni, penne or penne rigate

salt and ground black pepper

freshly grated Pecorino cheese, to serve

chopped flat leaf parsley, to garnish

Serves 4–6

1 Put the lentils in a medium saucepan, add 475ml/16fl oz/2 cups water and bring to the boil over a high heat. Lower the heat to a gentle simmer and cook, stirring occasionally, for 15–20 minutes or until the lentils are just tender. Meanwhile, soak the dried mushrooms in 175ml/6fl oz/$^3/4$ cup warm water for 15–20 minutes.

2 Tip the lentils into a sieve to drain, then rinse under the cold tap. Drain the soaked mushrooms and reserve the soaking liquid. Finely chop the mushrooms and set aside.

3 Heat the oil in a large saucepan and add the carrot, celery, onion, garlic, parsley and chillies, if using. Cook over a low heat, stirring constantly, for 5–7 minutes.

4 Add the stock, then the mushrooms and their soaking liquid. Bring to the boil, then add the beans, chick-peas and lentils, with salt and pepper to taste. Cover, and simmer gently for 20 minutes.

5 Add the pasta and bring the soup back to the boil, stirring. Simmer, stirring frequently, until the pasta is *al dente*: 7–8 minutes or according to the instructions on the packet. Season, then serve hot in soup bowls, with grated Pecorino and chopped parsley.

COOK'S TIP

If you like, you can freeze the soup at the end of Step 4. To serve, thaw and bring to the boil, then add the pasta and simmer until it is just tender.

Zuppa di Vongole e Pastina

Clam and Pasta Soup

SUBTLY SWEET AND SPICY, this soup is substantial enough to be served on its own for lunch or supper. A crusty Italian loaf such as pugliese is the ideal accompaniment.

INGREDIENTS

30ml/2 tbsp olive oil

1 onion, finely chopped

leaves from 1 fresh or dried thyme sprig, chopped, plus extra to garnish

2 garlic cloves, crushed

5–6 fresh basil leaves, plus extra to garnish

1.5–2.5ml/¼–½ tsp crushed red chillies, to taste

1 litre/1¾ pints/4 cups fish stock

350ml/12fl oz/1½ cups passata

5ml/1 tsp granulated sugar

90g/3½oz/scant 1 cup frozen peas

65g/2½oz/⅔ cup dried small pasta shapes, e.g. chifferini

225g/8oz frozen shelled clams or bottled clams in their shells

salt and ground black pepper

Serves 4–6

1 Heat the oil in a large saucepan, add the onion and cook gently for about 5 minutes until softened, but not coloured. Add the thyme, then stir in the garlic, basil leaves and chillies.

2 Add the stock, passata and sugar to the saucepan, with salt and pepper to taste. Bring to the boil, then lower the heat and simmer gently, stirring occasionally, for 15 minutes. Add the frozen peas and cook for a further 5 minutes.

3 Add the pasta to the stock and bring to the boil, stirring. Lower the heat and simmer, stirring frequently, until the pasta is only just *al dente*: about 5 minutes or according to the packet instructions.

4 Turn the heat down to low, add the frozen or bottled clams and heat through for 2–3 minutes. Taste for seasoning. Serve hot in warmed bowls, garnished with basil and thyme.

COOK'S TIP

Frozen shelled clams are available at good fishmongers and supermarkets; if you can't get them, use bottled or canned clams in natural juice (not vinegar). Italian delicatessens sell jars of clams in their shells. These both look and taste delicious and they are not too expensive. For a special occasion, stir some into the soup.

Minestrone di Orecchiette e Broccoli

Broccoli, Anchovy and Pasta Soup

THIS SOUP IS FROM PUGLIA in the south of Italy, where anchovies and broccoli are often used together.

INGREDIENTS

30ml/2 tbsp olive oil

I small onion, finely chopped

I garlic clove, finely chopped

1/4–1/3 fresh red chilli, seeded and
    finely chopped

2 drained canned anchovies

200ml/7fl oz/scant I cup passata

45ml/3 tbsp dry white wine

1.2 litres/2 pints/5 cups vegetable stock

300g/11oz/2 cups broccoli florets

200g/7oz/1¾ cups dried orecchiette

salt and ground black pepper

freshly grated Pecorino cheese,
    to serve

Serves 4

I Heat the oil in a large saucepan. Add the onion, garlic, chilli and anchovies and cook over a low heat, stirring all the time, for 5–6 minutes.

2 Add the passata and wine, with salt and pepper to taste. Bring to the boil, cover the pan, then cook over a low heat, stirring occasionally, for 12–15 minutes.

3 Pour in the stock. Bring to the boil, then add the broccoli and simmer for about 5 minutes. Add the pasta and bring back to the boil, stirring. Simmer, stirring frequently, until the pasta is *al dente*: 7–8 minutes or according to the instructions on the packet. Taste for seasoning. Serve hot, in warmed bowls. Hand around grated Pecorino separately.

Brodo di Quadrucci e Piselli

Pasta Squares and Peas in Broth

THIS THICK SOUP IS FROM LAZIO, where it is traditionally made with fresh home-made pasta and peas. In this modern version, ready-made pasta is used with frozen peas, to save time.

INGREDIENTS

25g/1oz/2 tbsp butter

50g/2oz pancetta or rindless smoked
    streaky bacon, roughly chopped

I small onion, finely chopped

I celery stick, finely chopped

400g/14oz/3½ cups frozen peas

5ml/1 tsp tomato purée

5–10ml/1–2 tsp finely chopped fresh flat
    leaf parsley

I litre/1¾ pints/4 cups chicken stock

300g/11oz fresh lasagne sheets

about 50g/2oz prosciutto crudo (Parma
    ham), cut into cubes

salt and ground black pepper

freshly grated Parmesan cheese, to serve

Serves 4–6

I Melt the butter in a large saucepan and add the pancetta or bacon, with the onion and celery. Cook over a low heat, stirring constantly, for 5 minutes.

2 Add the peas and cook, stirring, for 3–4 minutes. Stir in the tomato purée and parsley, then add the chicken stock, with salt and pepper to taste. Bring to the boil. Cover, lower the heat and simmer for 10 minutes. Meanwhile, cut the lasagne sheets into 2cm/¾in squares.

3 Taste the stock for seasoning. Drop in the pasta, stir and bring to the boil. Simmer for 2–3 minutes or until the pasta is *al dente*, then stir in the prosciutto. Serve hot in warmed bowls, with grated Parmesan handed around separately.

COOK'S TIP

Take care when adding salt, because of the saltiness of the pancetta and the prosciutto.

Zuppa di Fagioli con la Pasta

Bean and Pasta Soup

THIS HEARTY MAIN MEAL soup
sometimes goes by the simpler
name of *Pasta e Fagioli*, while some
Italians refer to it as *Minestrone di
Pasta e Fagioli*. Traditional country
recipes use dried beans and a ham
bone, and require the soup to be
cooked for a long time.

INGREDIENTS

1 onion

1 carrot

1 celery stick

30ml/2 tbsp olive oil

*115g/4oz pancetta or rindless smoked
    streaky bacon, diced*

1.75 litres/3 pints/7^1/2 cups beef stock

*1 cinnamon stick or a good pinch of
    ground cinnamon*

*90g/3^1/2oz/scant 1 cup dried pasta shapes,
    e.g. conchiglie or corallini*

*400g/14oz can borlotti beans, rinsed
    and drained*

*1 thick slice cooked ham, about
    225g/8oz, diced*

salt and ground black pepper

coarsely shaved Parmesan cheese, to serve

Serves 4–6

1 Chop the vegetables. Heat the oil in
a large saucepan, add the pancetta or
bacon and cook, stirring, until lightly
coloured. Add the chopped vegetable
mixture to the pan and cook for about
10 minutes, stirring frequently, until
lightly coloured. Pour in the stock, add
the cinnamon with salt and pepper to
taste, and bring to the boil. Cover and
simmer gently for 15–20 minutes.

2 Add the pasta. Bring back to the
boil, stirring all the time. Lower
the heat and simmer, stirring frequently,
for 5 minutes. Add the beans and diced
ham and simmer until the pasta is
al dente: 2–3 minutes or according to
the instructions on the packet.

3 Taste the soup for seasoning.
Serve hot in warmed bowls,
sprinkled with shavings of Parmesan.

VARIATIONS

• *Use spaghetti or tagliatelle instead of
the small pasta shapes, breaking it into
small pieces over the pan.*

• *Use cannellini or white haricot beans
instead of the borlotti. Alternatively, use
dried beans that have been soaked,
drained and boiled for 1 hour or until
tender. Add them to the pan after the
stock in Step 1.*

• *If you like, add 15ml/1 tbsp passata or
tomato purée, or 1 large ripe tomato,
skinned and chopped, with the beans
and diced ham.*

Pasta and Chick-pea Soup

A SIMPLE, COUNTRY-STYLE soup. The shape of the pasta and the beans complement one another beautifully.

INGREDIENTS

1 onion

2 carrots

2 celery sticks

60ml/4 tbsp olive oil

400g/14oz can chick-peas, rinsed and drained

200g/7oz can cannellini beans, rinsed and drained

150ml/¼ pint/⅔ cup passata

120ml/4fl oz/½ cup water

1.5 litres/2½ pints/6¼ cups vegetable or chicken stock

2 fresh or dried rosemary sprigs

200g/7oz/scant 2 cups dried conchiglie

salt and ground black pepper

freshly grated Parmesan cheese, to serve

Serves 4–6

1 Chop the onion, carrots and celery finely, either in a food processor or by hand.

2 Heat the oil in a large saucepan, add the chopped vegetable mixture and cook over a low heat, stirring frequently, for 5–7 minutes.

3 Add the chick-peas and cannellini beans, stir well to mix, then cook for 5 minutes. Stir in the passata and water. Cook, stirring, for 2–3 minutes.

4 Add 475ml/16fl oz/2 cups of the stock, one of the rosemary sprigs and salt and pepper to taste. Bring to the boil, cover, then simmer gently, stirring occasionally, for 1 hour.

5 Pour in the remaining stock, add the pasta and bring to the boil, stirring. Lower the heat and simmer, stirring frequently, until the pasta is *al dente*: 7–8 minutes or according to the instructions on the packet. Taste for seasoning. Remove the rosemary and serve the soup hot, in warmed bowls, topped with grated Parmesan and a few rosemary leaves.

VARIATIONS

• *You can use other pasta shapes, but conchiglie are ideal because they scoop up the chick-peas and beans.*

• *If you like, crush 1–2 garlic cloves and fry them with the vegetables.*

Minestrone alla Pugliese

Puglia-style Minestrone

THIS IS A TASTY SOUP for a Monday supper, because it can be made with the leftover carcass of Sunday's roast chicken. The sprinkling of salty ricotta salata at the finish is typical of Puglian cooking.

INGREDIENTS

1 roast chicken carcass

1 onion, quartered lengthways

1 carrot, roughly chopped

1 celery stick, roughly chopped

a few black peppercorns

1 small handful mixed fresh herbs, such as parsley and thyme

1 chicken stock cube

50g/2oz/^{1}/2 cup tubetti

salt and ground black pepper

50g/2oz ricotta salata, coarsely grated or crumbled and 30ml/2 tbsp fresh mint leaves, to serve

Serves 4

1 Break the chicken carcass into pieces and place these in a large saucepan. Add the onion, carrot, celery, pepper-corns and herbs, then crumble in the stock cube and add a good pinch of salt. Cover the chicken generously with cold water (you will need about 1.5 litres/2^1/2 pints/6^1/4 cups) and bring to the boil over a high heat.

2 Lower the heat, half cover the pan and simmer gently for about 1 hour. Remove the pan from the heat and leave to cool, then strain the liquid through a colander or sieve into a clean large saucepan.

3 Remove any meat from the chicken bones, cut it into bite-size pieces and set aside. Discard the carcass and flavouring ingredients.

4 Bring the stock in the pan to the boil, add the pasta and simmer, stirring frequently, until only just *al dente*: 5–6 minutes or according to the instructions on the packet.

5 Add the pieces of chicken and heat through for a few minutes, by which time the pasta will be ready. Taste for seasoning. Serve hot in warmed bowls, sprinkled with the ricotta salata and mint leaves.

COOK'S TIPS

• *Use other small, hollow pasta shapes, such as chifferini or pennette, for this soup, if you like.*

• *Ricotta salata is a salted and dried version of ricotta cheese. It is firmer than the traditional soft white ricotta, and can be easily diced, crumbled and even grated. It is available from some delicatessens, good cheese shops and large supermarkets. If you can't locate it, use feta cheese instead.*

Zuppa di Lenticchie e Pastina

Lentil and Pasta Soup

THIS RUSTIC VEGETARIAN soup makes a warming winter meal and goes well with granary or crusty Italian bread.

INGREDIENTS

175g/6oz/³/4 cup brown lentils

3 garlic cloves

1 litre/1³/4 pints/4 cups water

45ml/3 tbsp olive oil

25g/1oz/2 tbsp butter

1 onion, finely chopped

2 celery sticks, finely chopped

30ml/2 tbsp sun-dried tomato paste

1.75 litres/3 pints/7¹/2 cups vegetable stock

a few fresh marjoram leaves

a few fresh basil leaves

leaves from 1 fresh thyme sprig

50g/2oz/¹/2 cup dried small pasta shapes,
  e.g. tubetti

salt and ground black pepper

tiny fresh herb leaves, to garnish

Serves 4–6

COOK'S TIP

Use green lentils instead of brown if you like, but the orange or red ones go mushy.

1 Put the lentils in a large saucepan. Smash 1 garlic clove (there's no need to peel it first) and add it to the lentils. Pour in the water and bring to the boil. Lower the heat to a gentle simmer and cook, stirring occasionally, for about 20 minutes or until the lentils are just tender. Tip the lentils into a sieve, remove the garlic and set it aside. Rinse the lentils under the cold tap, then leave them to drain.

2 Heat 30ml/2 tbsp of the oil with half of the butter in a large saucepan. Add the onion and celery and cook over a low heat, stirring frequently, for 5–7 minutes until softened.

3 Crush the remaining garlic, then peel and mash the reserved garlic. Add to the vegetables with the remaining oil, the tomato paste and the lentils. Stir, then add the stock, the fresh herbs and salt and pepper to taste. Bring to the boil, stirring. Simmer for 30 minutes, stirring occasionally.

4 Add the pasta and bring the water back to the boil, stirring. Simmer, stirring frequently, until the pasta is *al dente*: 7–8 minutes or according to the packet instructions. Add the remaining butter and taste for seasoning. Serve hot in warmed bowls, sprinkled with the herb leaves.

Zuppa Casalinga

Farmhouse Soup

ROOT VEGETABLES FORM the base of this chunky, minestrone-style main meal soup. You can vary the vegetables according to what you have to hand.

INGREDIENTS

30ml/2 tbsp olive oil

1 onion, roughly chopped

3 carrots, cut into large chunks

175–200g/6–7oz turnips, cut into
  large chunks

about 175g/6oz swede, cut into
  large chunks

400g/14oz can chopped Italian tomatoes

15ml/1 tbsp tomato purée

5ml/1 tsp dried mixed herbs

5ml/1 tsp dried oregano

50g/2oz/½ cup dried peppers, washed and
  thinly sliced (optional)

1.5 litres/2½ pints/6¼ cups vegetable
  stock or water

50g/2oz/½ cup dried small macaroni
  or conchiglie

400g/14oz can red kidney beans, rinsed
  and drained

30ml/2 tbsp chopped fresh flat leaf parsley

salt and ground black pepper

freshly grated Parmesan cheese, to serve

Serves 4

1 Heat the oil in a large saucepan, add the onion and cook over a low heat for about 5 minutes until softened. Add the fresh vegetables, canned tomatoes, tomato purée, dried herbs and dried peppers, if using. Stir in salt and pepper to taste. Pour in the stock or water and bring to the boil. Stir well, cover, lower the heat and simmer for 30 minutes, stirring occasionally.

COOK'S TIP

Packets of dried Italian peppers are sold in many supermarkets and in delicatessens. They are piquant and firm with a "meaty" bite to them, which makes them ideal for adding substance to vegetarian soups.

2 Add the pasta and bring to the boil, stirring. Lower the heat and simmer, uncovered, until the pasta is only just *al dente*: about 5 minutes or according to the instructions on the packet. Stir frequently.

3 Stir in the beans. Heat through for 2–3 minutes, then remove from the heat and stir in the parsley. Taste the soup for seasoning. Serve hot in warmed soup bowls, with grated Parmesan handed separately.

Roasted Tomato and Pasta Soup

WHEN THE ONLY TOMATOES you can buy are not particularly flavoursome, make this soup. The oven-roasting compensates for any lack of flavour in the tomatoes, and the soup has a wonderful smoky taste.

INGREDIENTS

450g/1lb ripe Italian plum tomatoes, halved lengthways
1 large red pepper, quartered lengthways and seeded
1 large red onion, quartered lengthways
2 garlic cloves, unpeeled
15ml/1 tbsp olive oil
1.2 litres/2 pints/5 cups vegetable stock or water
good pinch of granulated sugar
90g/3¹/₂oz/scant 1 cup dried small pasta shapes, e.g. tubetti or small macaroni
salt and ground black pepper
fresh basil leaves, to garnish

Serves 4

1 Preheat the oven to 190°C /375°F/ Gas 5. Spread out the tomatoes, red pepper, onion and garlic in a roasting tin and drizzle with the olive oil. Roast for 30–40 minutes until the vegetables are soft and charred, stirring and turning them halfway.

2 Tip the vegetables into a food processor, add about 250ml/ 8fl oz/1 cup of the stock or water and process until puréed. Scrape into a sieve placed over a large saucepan and press the purée through into the pan.

3 Add the remaining stock or water, the sugar and salt and pepper to taste. Bring to the boil, stirring.

4 Add the pasta and simmer, stirring frequently, until *al dente*: 7–8 minutes or according to the instructions on the packet. Taste for seasoning. Serve hot in warmed bowls, garnished with the fresh basil.

COOK'S TIPS

• *You can roast the vegetables in advance, allow them to cool, then leave them in a covered bowl in the fridge overnight before puréeing.*
• *The soup can be frozen without the pasta. Thaw and bring to the boil before adding the pasta.*

Pasta Soups

Pasta Soup with Chicken Livers

A SOUP THAT CAN BE served as either a first or main course. The fried fegatini are so delicious that even if you do not normally like chicken livers you will find yourself loving them in this soup.

INGREDIENTS

115g/4oz/²/3 cup chicken livers, thawed
   if frozen
3 sprigs each fresh parsley, marjoram
   and sage
leaves from 1 fresh thyme sprig
5–6 fresh basil leaves
15ml/1 tbsp olive oil
knob of butter
4 garlic cloves, crushed
15–30ml/1–2 tbsp dry white wine
2 x 300g/11oz cans condensed
   chicken consommé
225g/8oz/2 cups frozen peas
50g/2oz/¹/2 cup dried pasta shapes,
   e.g. farfalle
2–3 spring onions, diagonally sliced
salt and ground black pepper
Serves 4–6

1 Cut the chicken livers into small pieces with scissors. Chop the herbs. Heat the oil and butter in a frying pan, add the garlic and herbs, with salt and pepper to taste, and fry gently for a few minutes. Add the livers, increase the heat to high and stir-fry for a few minutes until they change colour and become dry. Pour the wine over the livers, cook until the wine evaporates, then remove the livers from the heat and taste for seasoning.

2 Tip both cans of condensed chicken consommé into a large saucepan and add water to the condensed soup as directed on the labels. Add an extra can of water, then stir in a little salt and pepper to taste and bring to the boil.

3 Add the frozen peas to the pan and simmer for about 5 minutes, then add the small pasta shapes and bring the soup back to the boil, stirring. Allow to simmer, stirring frequently, until the pasta is only just *al dente*: about 5 minutes or according to the instructions on the packet.

4 Add the fried chicken livers and spring onions and heat through for 2–3 minutes. Taste for seasoning. Serve hot, in warmed bowls.

Meatball and Pasta Soup

EVEN THOUGH THIS SOUP comes from sunny Sicily, it is substantial enough for a hearty supper on a winter's day.

INGREDIENTS

2 x 300g/11oz cans condensed beef
*   consommé*
90g/3¹/₂oz/³/₄ cup dried very thin pasta,
*   e.g. fidelini or spaghettini*
fresh flat leaf parsley, to garnish
freshly grated Parmesan cheese, to serve

For the meatballs

1 very thick slice of white bread,
*   crusts removed*
30ml/2 tbsp milk
225g/8oz/1 cup minced beef
1 garlic clove, crushed
30ml/2 tbsp freshly grated
*   Parmesan cheese*
30–45ml/2–3 tbsp fresh flat leaf parsley
*   leaves, coarsely chopped*
1 egg
nutmeg
salt and ground black pepper

Serves 4

1 Make the meatballs. Break the bread into a small bowl, add the milk and set aside to soak. Meanwhile, put the minced beef, garlic, Parmesan, parsley and egg in another large bowl. Grate fresh nutmeg liberally over the top and add salt and pepper to taste.

2 Squeeze the bread with your hands to remove as much milk as possible, then add the bread to the meatball mixture and mix everything together well with your hands. Wash your hands, rinse them under the cold tap, then form the mixture into tiny balls about the size of small marbles.

3 Tip both cans of consommé into a large saucepan, add water as directed on the labels, then add an extra can of water. Stir in salt and pepper to taste and bring to the boil.

4 Drop in the meatballs, then break the pasta into small pieces and add it to the soup. Bring the soup to the boil, stirring gently. Simmer, stirring frequently, until the pasta is *al dente*: 7–8 minutes or according to the instructions on the packet. Taste for seasoning. Serve hot in warmed bowls, sprinkled with parsley and freshly grated Parmesan cheese.

Index

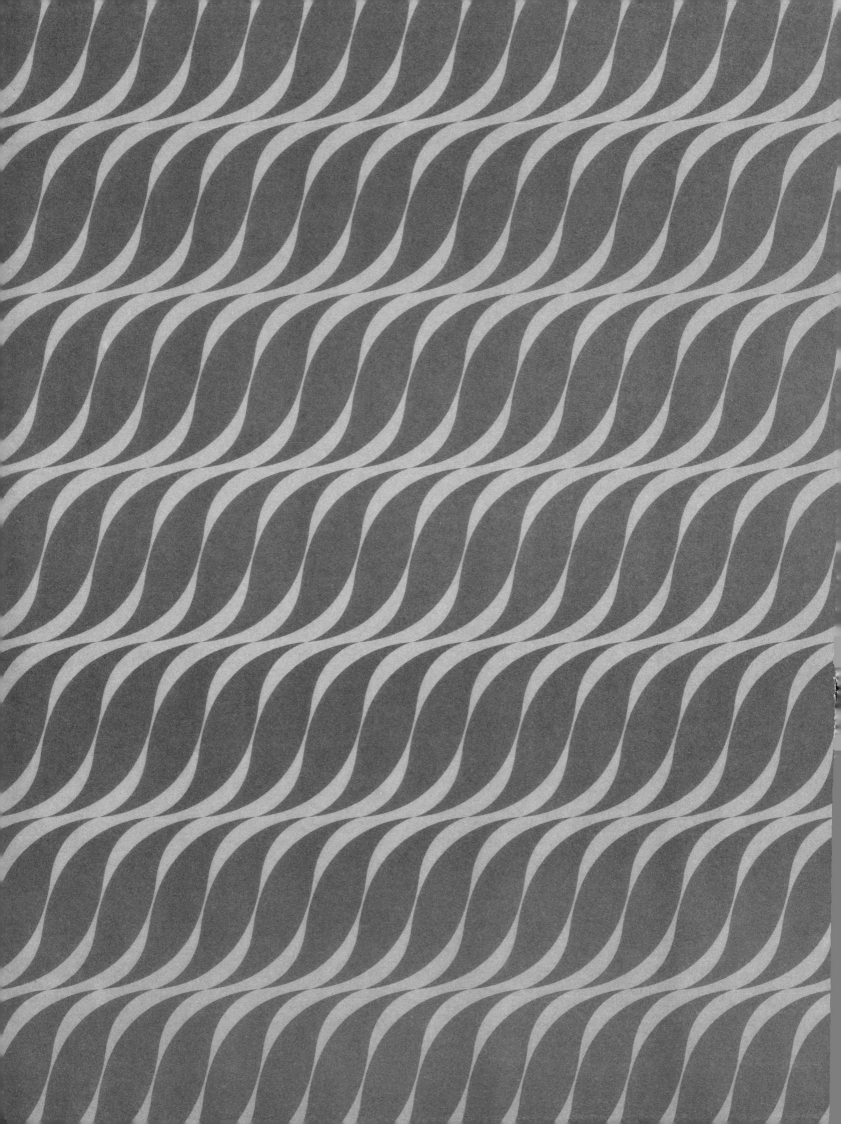